Improve Your
Punctuation & Grammar

If you want to know how . . .

Writing an Essay
How to improve your performance in coursework and examinations

Writing Your Dissertation
How to plan, prepare and present successful work

Handbook for Writers of English
Punctuation, common practice and usage

Writing Your Life Story
How to record and present your memories for future generations to enjoy

Improve Your Written English
Master the essentials of grammar, punctuation and spelling and write with great confidence

howtobooks

Please send for a free copy of the latest catalogue to:

How To Books
Spring Hill House, Spring Hill Road, Begbroke,
Oxford OX5 1RX, United Kingdom
email: info@howtobooks.co.uk
www.howtobooks.co.uk

Improve Your Punctuation & Grammar

Master the essentials of the English language, and write with greater confidence

2nd edition

MARION FIELD

howtobooks

Published by How To Books Ltd,
Spring Hill House, Spring Hill Road, Begbroke,
Oxford OX5 1RX, United Kingdom.
Tel: (01865) 375794. Fax: (01865) 379162.
email: info@howtobooks.co.uk
www.howtobooks.co.uk

First edition 2000
Reprinted 2000
Second edition 2003
Reprinted 2004
Reprinted 2005
Reprinted 2006 (twice)
Reprinted 2007

British Library Cataloguing in Publication Data.
A catalogue record for this book is available from
the British Library.

ISBN 13: 978 1 85703 873 6

Cover design by Baseline Arts Ltd, Oxford
Produced for How To Books by Deer Park Productions
Typeset by Kestrel Data, Exeter
Printed and bound by Cromwell Press Ltd, Trowbridge, Wiltshire

Contents

Preface
to the Second Edition

Do you have trouble with punctuation? Are you frustrated when you can't remember whether to use a comma or a full stop? Do you have difficulty constructing a sentence that sounds right? If so, then this book should help you. Written in an easy-to-read style, it takes you through the basics of English grammar. It explains the various parts of speech showing what role they each play in a sentence. It shows you how to improve your writing by choosing the right words and varying your sentence structure.

The use of the various punctuation marks is explained and examples given. After reading this book, you will never again use a comma instead of a full stop! There is a chapter on the use of apostrophes. You are shown how to write dialogue and even how to set out a play. There is a chapter on avoiding the most common mistakes. At the end of each chapter there are exercises which will help to reinforce what you have learnt.

Written in a simple style with frequent headings, this book is for anyone – of any age – who wishes to improve the standard of his or her English.

Marion Field

1

Grammatical Guidelines

The organisation of language is known as grammar. Every word in the English language is a particular **part of speech** and has a name by which to identify it. Some parts of speech *must* be included in a sentence for it to make sense. Others are used to enhance your writing and make it interesting to read. The parts of speech that are *essential* for every sentence are **nouns** (or **pronouns**) and **verbs**.

DIFFERENT TYPES OF NOUNS

Nouns are the names of things or people. There are different types of nouns but you must include at least one noun or one pronoun in each sentence you write. There will be more about pronouns later.

Concrete or common nouns

A **concrete** or **common noun** is the name given to a physical thing – something that can be seen:

book	cake	dog	elephant
fire	garage	hair	jewel
key	letter	needle	orchid
parchment	queen	recipe	sailor
tattoo	volunteer	watch	zoo

Forming plurals

A noun is singular if it refers to one thing. Plural means there is more than one of the item. To make a concrete noun plural, it is usually necessary to add an 's' at the end of the word:

Singular	*Plural*
bone	bones
dog	dogs
ear	ears
friend	friends
simile	similes
metaphor	metaphors
zoo	zoos

Words that end in 'ch', 's', 'sh' and 'z' have to add 'es' for ease of pronunciation:

Singular	*Plural*
bush	bushes
buzz	buzzes
crutch	crutches
church	churches
dash	dashes
duchess	duchesses
flash	flashes
princess	princesses
witness	witnesses

Some words keep the same word for the plural as the singular:

Singular	*Plural*
cod	cod
deer	deer
salmon	salmon
sheep	sheep

Other words change the form of the word as in the following:

Singular	Plural
child	children
foot	feet
goose	geese
ox	oxen
man	men
tooth	teeth
woman	women

All words are composed of **vowels** (a, e, i, o, u) and **consonants** (all other letters). Words that end in 'y' preceded by a consonant change the 'y' to an 'i' before adding 'es':

Singular	Plural
ally	allies
county	counties
cry	cries
enemy	enemies
reply	replies

Some nouns that end in 'f' or 'fe' change the ending to 'ves' to make the plural:

Singular	Plural
half	halves
knife	knives
wolf	wolves

Unfortunately some words ending in 'f' keep it before adding an 's':

Singular	Plural
hoof	hoofs
proof	proofs

For the following word you have a choice:

dwarf   dwarfs or dwarves

Proper nouns

A proper noun is the name of a person, a place or a particular thing or institution. It *always* starts with a capital letter.

Names of people

| Alice | Bernard | Betty | Clive |
| Elizabeth | Lennie | Lucy | Richard |

Titles are also written with a capital letter:

Mrs Alexander	Mr Bell
Prince Edward	The Earl of Northumberland
Lady Thatcher	The Countess of Wessex
The Duchess of York	

Names of places

England	Guildford	Hampshire	London
River Thames	Mount Everest	The Forest of Dean	
The Lake District			

Names of buildings and institutions

The British Broadcasting Corporation	The British Museum
Buckingham Palace	Cleopatra's Needle
Nelson's Column	The Royal Academy
The Royal Air Force	The United Nations
Windsor Castle	

Religious names

All proper nouns connected with religion start with capital letters.

Bible	Christian	Christianity	Christmas
Easter	Eid	Judaism	Jew
Hanukka	Hindu	Islam	Koran

Abstract nouns

An abstract noun is more vague. It refers to a quality, an idea, a state of mind, an occasion, a feeling or a time. It cannot be seen or touched. The following are all abstract nouns:

anger	beauty	birth	brightness
criticism	comfort	darkness	excellence
happiness	health	jealousy	month
patience	peace	pregnancy	war

Collective nouns

Collective nouns are nouns that refer to a group of objects or people. Although they represent a number of things, they are singular words as they can be made plural.

Singular	*Plural*
class	classes
choir	choirs
collection	collections
congregation	congregations
crew	crews
crowd	crowds
flock	flocks
group	groups
herd	herds
orchestra	orchestras
team	teams

Verbal nouns or gerunds

The form of the verb known as the present participle always ends in 'ing'. As well as being used as a verb, this form can also be used as a noun. It is called a gerund or verbal noun. Look at the following sentences which use gerunds.

I like <u>shopping</u>.

The baby's <u>crying</u> annoyed her.

The <u>howling</u> of the wolves kept the hunters awake.

The <u>growling</u> of the guard dog terrified the burglars.

The pianist's <u>playing</u> was superb.

Subjects and objects

The **subject** of the sentence is the noun or pronoun that is the main reason for the sentence. It performs the action.

The <u>boy</u> ran across the road.

'The boy' is the **subject** of the sentence.

The **object** of a sentence is the noun or pronoun to which something is done.

Lucy played the <u>piano</u>.

The 'piano' is the **object** of the sentence. A sentence *must* contain a subject but there does not have to be an object in the sentence. The following sentence does not contain an object:

Lucy plays very well.

THE ARTICLES

There are three articles:

the   a   an

'The' is the **definite article** as it refers to a specific thing.

The dress you made is beautiful.

'A' and 'an' are **indefinite articles** and are used more gener-
ally.

Cathy is going to make a dress.

'An' is also an indefinite article and is used before a vowel
for ease of pronunciation.

I saw an elephant today.

PRONOUNS

A **pronoun** is a word that replaces a noun, a noun phrase or
a noun clause. There will be more about phrases and clauses
later. Each sentence must contain at least one noun *or* one
pronoun.

Personal pronouns

Personal pronouns take the place of nouns, noun phrases
and noun clauses. They are known as the first, second and
third persons. They can be used as both subjects and objects
within your sentence. Look at the following table.

	Singular		*Plural*	
	Subject	*Object*	*Subject*	*Object*
First person	I	me	we	us
Second person	you	you	you	you
Third person	he	him	they	them
	she	her	they	them
	it	it	they	them

Notice that the second person is the same in both the singular and plural. In the past *thou* (subject) and *thine* (object) was used as the singular but today *you* is in general use for both although you may still hear *thou* in some parts of the country.

Nouns can be replaced with personal pronouns

So that a noun is not repeated too frequently, a *personal* pronoun is often used to replace it. Look at the following sentence:

Sarah was annoyed that Sarah was not allowed to go to the party.

Obviously this sentence would be better if the second 'Sarah' was replaced by 'she'.

Sarah was annoyed that she was not allowed to go to the party.

'She' is the subject of the second part of the sentence.

Tracy went to the party. She enjoyed the party.

This sentence would be better if 'party' was not used twice.

Tracy went to the party. She enjoyed it.

'It' is the object of the second sentence.

When writing, check that you don't repeat nouns unnecessarily. Replace them with pronouns.

Demonstrative pronouns

Demonstrative pronouns can also replace nouns. The demonstrative pronouns are:

> *Singular*:   this   that
> *Plural*:   these   those

This is their house.

In the above sentence 'this' stands for 'their house'.

Those are his cattle.

'Those' replaces 'his cattle'.

'This', 'that', 'these' and 'those' can also be used as adjectives if they are attached to a noun. There will be more about this in a later chapter.

Possessive pronouns

Possessive pronouns also replace nouns and indicate that something 'belongs'. They are related to the personal pronouns.

		Personal	*Possessive*
First person	– singular	I	mine
	– plural	we	ours
Second person	– singular	you	yours
	– plural	you	yours
Third person	– singular	he	his
		she	hers
		it	its
	– plural	they	theirs

This book is <u>mine</u>.

<u>Yours</u> is the blame.

The prize was <u>his</u>.

That new house is <u>theirs</u>.

Reflexive pronouns

Reflexive pronouns are used when the subject and the object of the sentence refer to the same person or thing. They 'reflect' the subject.

	Personal pronouns	*Reflexive pronouns*
First person singular	I	myself
Second person singular	you	yourself
Third person singular	he	himself
	she	herself
	it	itself
First person plural	we	ourselves
Second person plural	you	yourselves
Third person plural	they	themselves

I washed <u>myself</u> thoroughly.

The cat licked <u>itself</u> all over.

You mustn't blame <u>yourself</u>.

Notice that the reflexive third person plural pronoun is *themselves* not *theirselves*.

They wore <u>themselves</u> out.

not

They wore <u>theirselves</u> out.

Intensive pronouns

Intensive pronouns are the same words as reflexive pronouns but are used for emphasis.

He, <u>himself</u>, presented the prizes.

I wrote it <u>myself</u>.

It is *not* correct to use this form of the pronoun when the object does not reflect the subject.

That house belongs to <u>myself</u>.

This is incorrect. It should be:

That house belongs to <u>me</u>.

Interrogative pronouns

Interrogative pronouns are used to ask a question and are usually at the beginning of a sentence. They are:

     which   who   whom   whose

<u>Which</u> will you wear?

<u>Who</u> is that boy?

To <u>whom</u> are you speaking?

<u>Whose</u> is that?

> **Do remember to put a question mark at the end of your sentence**.

FINITE AND NON-FINITE VERBS

Verbs are the 'doing' or 'being' words in a sentence. Without them your work will make no sense. There is one 'being' verb, the verb 'to be'; the rest are 'doing' verbs. The verb 'to be' and the verb 'to have' are often joined with other words to change the tense. They are known as **auxiliary verbs**. The verb 'to do' can also sometimes be used as an auxiliary verb and placed before another verb.

The truant <u>was running</u> down the street.

The child <u>has fallen</u> over.

She <u>did bake</u> a cake for the competition.

Finite verbs

For a sentence to make sense it must contain a **finite verb** as well as the noun or pronoun which is the subject of the sentence. The verb must show '**person**' (first, second or third), **number** (singular or plural) and **tense** (past, present or future). A finite verb changes its form depending on the tense. Look at the following sentence:

Mary drew a picture.

'Mary' (third person– she) is the subject of the sentence. The verb 'drew' has a '**person**' connected to it, 'Mary', who is singular (**number**), and 'drew' is the past **tense** of the verb 'to draw'. Therefore it is a finite verb. It would also be a finite verb in the present tense:

Mary draws a picture.

> **All sentences must contain at least one finite verb**.

Non-finite verbs

Non-finite verbs *never* change their form. The non-finite parts of the verbs are:

◆ the base form of the verb: write, dance

◆ the infinitive – the verb introduced by 'to': to be, to write, to dance

◆ the present participle which always ends in 'ing': writing, dancing

◆ the past participle which sometimes ends in 'ed' but has exceptions as many verbs are irregular.

The present and past participles

The present and the past participles of 'doing' verbs can be used with the auxiliary verbs 'to be' and 'to have'. This will change the form of the verb and make a finite verb. A verb sometimes consists of more than one word.

Present and past tenses of the verb 'to be'

	Present tense	*Past tense*
I	am	was
you	are	were
he, she, it	is	was
we	are	were
they	are	were

Present and past tenses of the verb 'to have'

I	have	had
you	have	had
he, she, it	has	had
we	have	had
they	have	had

The present participle

The present participle of the verb can be used with the verb 'to be' to form the present and past 'progressive' tenses. This suggests that the action is still continuing. The participle remains the same but the tense of the verb 'to be' changes.

The present progressive tense using the present participle 'writing'

I am writing.

You are writing.

He, she is writing.

We are writing.

They are writing.

The past progressive tense using 'writing'

I <u>was writing</u>.

You <u>were writing</u>.

He, she <u>was writing</u>.

We <u>were writing</u>.

They <u>were writing</u>.

Both the present progressive and the past progressive tenses use the *present* participle *not* the *past*. Mistakes are often made with the verb 'to sit'.

I was <u>sat</u> in my place.

This is wrong. 'Sat' is the *past* participle of the verb to 'to sit' and should be used with the verb 'to have' *not* 'to be'. The sentence *should* read:

I was <u>sitting</u> in my place.   (verb 'to be' + the present participle)

or

I <u>had sat</u> in my place. (verb 'to have' + the past participle)

The progressive aspect of the verb can also be used in the perfect tense. This also suggests a continuous action. In this case the past participle of the verb 'to be', 'been' is placed with the verb 'to have' and the verb that is being used.

Present perfect progressive tense

The baby <u>has been crying</u> all day.

Past perfect progressive

The student <u>had been working</u> hard all summer.

The past participle

The past participle of a verb is often the same as the ordinary past tense and ends in 'ed'. It can be used with the verb 'to have' to form the present perfect tense and the past perfect tense. The present perfect tense uses the present tense of the verb 'to have' and the past perfect uses the past tense.

Present perfect tense	*Past perfect tense*
I have danced	I had danced
you have danced	you had danced
he, she has danced	he, she had danced
we have danced	we had danced
they have danced	they had danced

The past participle will have a different ending from '-ed' if it is an irregular verb.

Present perfect tense	*Past perfect tense*
I have written	I had written
You have written	You had written
He has written	She had written
We have written	We had written
They have written	They had written

The following table shows some of the irregular verbs:

Base form	*Infinitive*	*Present participle*	*Past participle*
be	to be	being	been
build	to build	building	built
do	to do	doing	done
drink	to drink	drinking	drunk
fling	to fling	flinging	flung

go	to go	going	gone
know	to know	knowing	known
see	to see	seeing	seen
speak	to swim	swimming	swum
wear	to wear	wearing	worn
write	to write	writing	written

> Use 'to be' with the *present* participle.
> Use 'to have' with the *past* participle.

Phrases

If you have only non-finite parts of the verb – base form, infinitive, present and past participles, in your work, you are *not* writing in sentences. The following examples are phrases because they do not contain a finite verb. There will be more about phrases in the next chapter.

Leap a hurdle

To be a teacher

Running across the road

Written a letter

None of the above has a subject and the participles 'running' and 'written' need parts of the verbs 'to be' or 'to have' added to them. A sentence *must* have a subject. The previous examples have none. A subject must be added. Look at the revised sentences.

She leapt the hurdle.

A subject 'she' has been added and 'leapt' is the past tense.

John wanted to be a teacher.

'John' is the subject and 'wanted' is the *finite* verb. It has person, number and tense so this *is* a sentence.

She was running across the road.

The subject is 'she' and 'was' has been added to the present participle to make the past progressive tense. The finite verb is 'was running'.

He has written a letter.

'He' is the third person and 'has' has been added to the past participle to make the perfect tense. The finite verb is 'has written'.

A finite verb can be more than one word.

Tenses

Finite verbs show tense – past, present and future.

The present and past tenses
The past tense often ends in 'ed'. Notice that the third person singular in the present tense usually ends in 's'.

To play

Present tense	*Past tense*
I play	I played
you play	you played
he, she, it plays	he, she, it played
we play	we played
they play	they played

There are however, many exceptions where the past tense does not end in 'ed'. Following are some of the verbs which have irregular past tenses. As with verbs that end in 'ed', the word remains the same for all persons.

Infinitive	Past tense
to build	built
to do	did
to drink	drank
to fling	flung
to grow	grew
to hear	heard
to know	knew
to leap	leapt
to swim	swam
to tear	tore
to write	wrote

The past and perfect tenses

Your essays and short stories will usually be written in the past tense. For the purpose of your writing, this will be the time at which the actions are taking place. If you wish to go further back in time, you will have to use the past perfect tense. Look at the following example:

He <u>looked</u> at the letter. Taking another one from the drawer, he <u>compared</u> the handwriting. It was the same. He <u>had received</u> the first letter a week ago.

'Looked' and 'compared' are the past tense because the actions are taking place 'now' in terms of the passage. 'Had received' is the past perfect tense because the action is further back in time.

The future tense

When writing the future tense of the verb, use 'shall' with the first person and 'will' with the second and third person.

I <u>shall</u> go to London tomorrow.

<u>You will</u> work hard at school.

<u>Mark will</u> write to you this evening.

<u>That tree will shed</u> its leaves in the aturum.

<u>We shall win</u> the match.

<u>They will move</u> house next month.

However, sometimes 'shall' and 'will' can change places for emphasis.

I <u>will</u> go to London tomorrow. (This suggests determination)

You <u>shall</u> go to the ball, Cinderella. (It will be made possible)

Present participle and infinitive

The verb 'to be' followed by the present participle 'going' is also used to express the future tense. It is followed by the infinitive of the appropriate verb. The use of this is becoming more common.

I <u>am going to start</u> writing a novel.

They <u>are going to visit</u> their mother.

Sometimes the verb 'to be' followed by the present participle also indicates the future.

The train <u>is leaving</u> in five minutes.

The film <u>is starting</u> soon.

The future progressive
As with the present progressive and the past progressive tenses, the future progressive also uses the present participle.

I <u>shall be visiting</u> her next week.

The Browns <u>will be buying</u> a dog soon.

Direct and indirect objects

There are both **direct** and **indirect objects**. If there is only one object in a sentence, it will be a direct object and will have something 'done to it' by the subject.

Tom scored a <u>goal</u> (direct object).

Judy ate her <u>lunch</u> (direct object).

Sometimes there are two objects as in the following sentences:

She gave <u>me</u> some <u>sweets</u>.

He threw <u>Mary</u> the <u>ball</u>.

'Sweets' and 'ball' are both direct objects. 'Me' and 'Mary' are indirect objects. The word 'to' is 'understood' before them.

She gave (to) me the sweets.

He threw (to) Mary the ball.

Complements

If the word at the end of the sentence refers directly to the subject, it is known as the **complement** and the preceding verb will usually be the verb 'to be'.

Joan (subject) is a nurse (complement).

Michael (subject) was the winner of the race (complement).

Transitive and intransitive verbs

Verbs that are followed by an object are called **transitive verbs**. Those that have no object are **intransitive**. Some verbs can be used both transitively and intransitively.

Transitive verbs

If there is an object in the sentence, the verb is transitive.

He threw the ball.

'The ball' is the object and therefore the verb 'threw' is transitive.

The doctor examined the patient.

'The patient' is the object. The verb 'examined' is transitive.

Intransitive verbs
If the verb is not followed by an object, then it is an **intransitive verb**.

She <u>dances</u> beautifully.

He <u>writes</u> very neatly.

There is no object in either of these sentences so both 'dances' and 'writes' are intransitive.

Verbs that are both transitive and intransitive
Many verbs can be used both transitively and intransitively. It depends on how they are used in the sentence.

He wrote a letter. (transitive: 'letter' is the object.)

She writes beautifully. (intransitive. There is no object.)

Joe swam a length. (transitive: 'length' is the object.)

The girls swam quickly. (intransitive. There is no object.)

The active or passive voice
Look at these two sentences:

His mother scolded Tom. (Active voice)

Tom was scolded by his mother. (Passive voice)

In the first sentence the mother is doing the action. This is called the **active voice**. In the second sentence Tom has something done to him. This is known as the **passive voice**. Both are acceptable but you can choose which is more suitable for the work you are writing. The active voice is commonly used as it has a more direct effect and usually uses fewer words. However, there are certain situations where the passive voice is more appropriate. Look at the following sentence:

The traitor was condemned to death.

The important person here is the traitor. We are not interested in *who* condemned him to death.

INTERJECTIONS

Interjections have no particular part to play in the sentence. They can express disgust, surprise, fear, fatigue, elation, boredom or some other emotion. Some examples are:

ah	eh	oh	er	hello
well	really			

They can sometimes be more than one word and are often followed by exclamation marks:

Oh dear!	What a pity!	Oh no!	Dear, dear!

CHECKLIST

◆ Nouns are the names of things.

◆ Proper nouns always start with a capital letter.

◆ Pronouns take the place of nouns.

◆ Verbs are 'doing' or 'being' words.

◆ A sentence *must* contain at least one noun or pronoun and one finite verb.

EXERCISES

1. Write the plurals of the following words:

cat	crutch	child	deer
duchess	dwarf	half	lady
man	marriage	metaphor	simile

2. In the passage identify all the following:

concrete nouns	proper nouns	abstract nouns
collective nouns	gerunds	finite verbs
personal pronouns	demonstrative pronouns	
possessive pronouns	interrogative pronouns	

Jenny decided to go to the town. She had suffered a bout of depression the day before when she had been in the audience at the local theatre. One of the actors had collapsed. She thought a day's shopping would be therapy for her. That had helped her in the past. It started to rain hard and she went to a cafe for a coffee. She left her umbrella in the stand. When she left, there were several umbrellas and she couldn't remember which was hers. Which one was it?

3. In the following passage, identify the non-finite and finite verbs.

Jo was bored. He wanted to play football but it was raining. Staring gloomily out of the window, he looked in vain for some blue sky. Annoyed, he picked up his latest football magazine to see if he could do the crossword.

4. In the following sentences identify the complements, direct objects and indirect objects

   (a) The teacher gave Jack a library book to read.
   (b) She wrote several letters while she was waiting.
   (c) He bought an ice cream at the kiosk near the beach.
   (d) She gave him an apple.
   (e) Their headmaster became an inspector.
   (f) Peter is a good swimmer.

5. In the following sentences which verbs are used transitively and which intransitively?

   (a) The baby cried all day.
   (b) He gave a lecture about the eclipse.
   (c) He threw the ball accurately at the wicket.
   (d) She is always talking.

6. Change the following sentences to the passive voice.

   (a) The hostess served the guest of honour first.
   (b) The landlord installed night storage heaters for his tenants.

See page 160 for suggested answers.

Sentence Construction

Words must be combined in a certain way to form sentences. This is known as **syntax**. In the previous chapter it was established that each sentence must contain a subject (noun or pronoun) and a finite verb (showing person, number and tense). However, your writing will be very monotonous if you use only this pattern and do not vary your sentence construction. There are many different forms you can use. Sections of your sentences that contain finite verbs and are linked together are called **clauses**. There are two types – main and subordinate. They will be explained in detail later.

THE SIMPLE SENTENCE

A sentence that consists of a subject and a finite verb is known as a **simple sentence**. This is a grammatical term and has nothing to do with the content of the sentence. It may contain additional words or phrases (groups of words that do not contain a finite verb). It consists of one main clause.

Subject and predicate

The simple sentence can be divided into two parts – the **subject** and the rest of the sentence called the **predicate**.

Subject	*Predicate*
The boy	ran across the road.
The stream	trickled along beside the path.
Jack	is an electrician.
She	gave me my wages.

A variety of phrases and clauses can be used to enhance your writing.

PHRASES

Phrases are groups of two or more words that do *not* contain a finite verb. They do not make sense on their own but add detail to the sentence. Phrases can do the same work as parts of speech. There are adjectival phrases, adverbial phrases and noun phrases. There will be more about adjectives and adverbs later. There are also prepositional phrases, participial phrases and infinitive phrases. Some phrases can be classified under two headings.

In the above sentences 'across the road' and 'beside the path' are both phrases. They don't make sense by themselves but they can be used as the subject, object or the complement of the sentence. They are sometimes introduced by a non-finite verb – the infinitive or the present or past participle.

Infinitive phrases

The infinitive is the part of the verb introduced by 'to'. An **infinitive phrase** is introduced by the infinitive.

To be a nurse was her ambition.

'To be a nurse' is an infinitive phrase as it starts with the infinitive 'to be'. It is also a noun phrase as it functions as the **subject** of the sentence.

She was <u>to become a popular teacher</u>.

'To become a popular teacher' is an infinitive phrase as it starts with the infinitive 'to become'. It is also a noun phrase as it acts as the **complement** of the sentence.

<u>To be a doctor</u> was his ambition.

'To be a doctor' is a phrase using the infinitive 'to be'. In this case the whole phrase is the **subject** of the main clause and 'ambition' is the **complement**.

Participial phrases

A **participial phrase** is introduced by a past or present participle.

<u>Running quickly across the road</u>, she stumbled.

The present participle 'running' introduces the phrase and so it is a participial phrase.

<u>Leaping out of bed</u>, he ran to the window.

This sentence starts with the present participle 'leaping' and is therefore a **participial phrase**. It adds detail to the sentence and is followed by a comma.

<u>Handcuffed to a policeman</u>, the prisoner was led away.

'Handcuffed' is the past participle and introduces the phrase which also functions as an adjectival phrase qualifying the noun 'prisoner'.

Gripped by fear, she stared at her questioner.

'Gripped' is the past participle and 'gripped by fear' is also a participial phrase.

Adjectival phrases

Like adjectives, **adjectival phrases** modify (describe) nouns or pronouns.

The man, tall and elegant, walked on to the platform.

'. . . tall and elegant' is an adjectival phrase modifying the noun 'man'.

The crowd, becoming upset, was ready to riot.

'. . . becoming upset' is an adjectival phrase qualifying the noun 'crowd'.

The headmaster, furiously angry, strode on to the platform.

'. . . furiously angry' is an adjectival phrase which describes the headmaster. There will be more about adjectives in the next chapter.

Adverbial phrases

Like adverbs, adverbial phrases answer the questions: how?
when? why? where?

They have gone <u>to France</u>. (where)

(Adverbial phrase of place and also a prepositional phrase.)

A total eclipse took place <u>on 11 August 1999</u>. (when)

(Adverbial phrase of time and also a prepositional phrase.)

He was driving <u>much too quickly</u>. (how)

(Adverbial phrase qualifying 'was driving'.)

<u>Exhausted by the heat</u>, she sat down in the shade. (why)

(Adverbial phrase of reason and also a participial phrase.)

Adverbial phrases can indicate:

Place
She waited <u>in the restaurant</u>.

The letter was <u>on the table</u>.

He stood <u>by the gate</u>.

Direction
He walked <u>across the road</u>.

The boy walked moodily <u>along the path</u>.

The train hurtled <u>through the tunnel</u>.

Time
The play finished <u>at ten o'clock</u>.

She worked <u>after lunch</u>.

The train left <u>on time</u>.

Noun phrases
Noun phrases are groups of words that can serve as subjects, objects, or complements in your sentence.

<u>The dark clouds overhead</u> suggested rain.

'The dark clouds overhead' is a noun phrase that is the **subject** of the sentence. This could be replaced by a pronoun.

<u>They</u> suggested rain.

The visitors admired <u>the elegant beauty of the house</u>.

'. . . the elegant beauty of the house' is the object of the sentence and could be replaced by the pronoun 'it'.

The visitors admired <u>it</u>.

<u>The school's football team</u> won the match.

'The school's football team' is the **subject** of the sentence.

She refused <u>to play tennis</u>.

'. . . to play tennis' is the **object** of the sentence. It is also an infinitive phrase.

Her ambition was <u>to write a novel</u>.

'. . . to write a novel' is the **complement** of the sentence. It refers to 'ambition'. It is also an infinitive phrase.

Using a gerundive phrase
A gerund is the present participle used as a noun. A **gerundive phrase** begins with a gerund.

<u>Swimming every day</u> helped him to recover.

'Swimming' is a gerund and 'Swimming every day' is the subject of the sentence.

Prepositions
A **preposition** is a word that indicates the relationship of a noun or pronoun to some other part of the sentence. The word 'preposition' means to be 'placed before'. Prepositions are usually placed before the noun and are often used in phrases.

Some prepositions are:

above	after	at	before	by	down
for	from	in	into	near	on
opposite	past	towards	through	to	under
with	without				

Some of these words can also be used as other parts of speech. It will depend on their role in the sentence.

Prepositional phrases.

A **prepositional phrase** begins with a preposition. In the following sentences the prepositions, followed by nouns, form phrases and are underlined.

Cautiously, they crept into the room.

She placed the book on the table.

The clouds moved across the sky.

Most prepositional phrases can be identified as other phrases as well. The above sentences are all adverbial phrases as they say *where* something happened. There will be more about adverbs later. Look at the following sentences.

The treasure was buried under the apple tree.

'. . . under the apple tree' is a prepositional phrase as it begins with a preposition. It is also an adverbial phrase of place as it says *where* the treasure was buried.

The house, by the lake, belongs to Lord Melton.

'. . . by the lake' begins with the preposition 'by' and so is a prepositional phrase. However it is also an adjectival phrase as it describes the lake.

Phrasal verbs

Phrasal verbs are verbs that are followed by a preposition which is part of the meaning of the verb. The preposition *can* be separated from the verb but this often produces a clumsy construction so it is better to keep them together. In most cases they *have* to be kept together or the sense is lost. Some examples are:

clear off	clear up	fall over	fly away
kick off	jump up	pick up	run away
throw away			

He <u>jumped up</u> in alarm.

She <u>threw away</u> the wrapping paper.

When the baby <u>fell over</u>, she cried.

The boy <u>ran away</u> from school.

MAIN CLAUSES

A simple sentence contains one **main clause** which can be constructed in various ways. However, it must contain only *one finite verb*. A main clause can be constructed in various ways. Some are suggested below.

Subject and finite verb

It (subject) rained (finite verb).

Subject, finite verb and direct object

Kay (subject) watched (finite verb) television (direct object).

Subject, finite verb, indirect object and direct object

His parents (subject) gave (finite verb) Brian (ind. object) a bike (dir. object).

Subject, finite verb and complement

The trickle of water (subject) became (finite verb) a deluge (complement).

Phrase, subject, finite verb, direct object and phrase

Fielding the ball (phrase), he (subject) threw (finite verb) it (direct object) at the wicket (phrase).

List of main clauses

David was doing his homework, Mary was playing the piano, Tony was cooking the dinner and Sue was feeding the baby.

Each of the above main clauses is separated by a comma and the last one is preceded by 'and'.

Main clauses joined by conjunctions

Two or more main clauses can be joined together to make a **compound sentence**. To do this you will need to use one of the **co-ordinating conjunctions** 'and', 'but', 'or'. **Conjunctions (connectives)** are joining words used to link clauses, phrases and words together.

Co-ordinating conjunctions

Simple sentences are all main clauses because they contain only one finite verb. If there is more than one finite verb in your sentence, you will have more than one clause. Check that you have used a conjunction to join them. In each of the following sentences there are two main clauses which have been linked with a co-ordinating conjunction. They are compound sentences.

(The teacher shouted) and (the class fell silent).

(Jane may go to the party) but (you will remain at home).

(You will do your homework) or (you will not be allowed to go out).

The co-ordinating conjunctions can also be used to link items and introduce phrases.

◆ hat *and* coat

◆ a raincoat *but* no umbrella

◆ London *or* Paris

He heard the tramp of feet *and* <u>the shouts of the men</u>. (phrase)

There was paper *but* <u>no sign of a pen</u>. (phrase)

You can use that book *or* <u>this collection of newspapers</u>. (phrase)

Do *not* use commas to separate *two* main clauses.

SUBORDINATE CLAUSES

Subordinate clauses are linked to a main clause by **subordinating conjunctions**. A sentence that contains main clauses and subordinate clauses is known as a **complex sentence**.

Subordinating conjunctions

Subordinating conjunctions are used to link main clauses to subordinate clauses. Some of them are:

after	although	as	because	before
if	since	that	though	unless
until	when	while		

The conjunction can go between the two clauses.

(They played tennis) although (it had started to rain).

(She went to the supermarket) because (she had run out of milk).

The conjunction can also be placed at the beginning of the sentence. In this case the subordinate clause comes first and a comma separates the two clauses.

Although (it had started to rain), (they played tennis).

Because (she had run out of milk), (she went to the supermarket).

> **If you begin a sentence with a subordinating conjunction, you *must* follow this with *two* clauses and put a comma between them.**

Subordinate clauses

There are a variety of subordinate clauses you can use. They have the same role as parts of speech.

Adverbial clauses

There are a variety of adverbial clauses. The type depends on their function in the sentence.

Adverbial clauses of time

An **adverbial clause of time** will indicate *when* an event happened. Remember that it *must* contain a subject (possibly 'understood') and a finite verb.

The traffic started to move when <u>the police had cleared the road</u>.

In the above sentence the adverbial clause of time could stand alone. The subject is 'police' and 'had cleared' is the finite verb. The clause tells us *when* the traffic started to move.

As <u>the shadow of the moon moved across the sun</u>, it became very dark.

When <u>the children had left</u>, she cleared up the remains of the party.

'. . . the shadow of the moon moved across the sun' and 'the children had left' are adverbial clauses of time saying *when* something happened.

Adverbial clauses of place

Adverbial clauses of place show *where* something took place. They are often introduced by the word 'where'.

A flourishing town grew up where <u>once a bomb had been dropped</u>.

I can't remember where <u>I left my bag</u>.

'. . . once a bomb had been dropped' and 'I left my bag' are both adverbial clauses of place linked to the main clauses by 'where'. They say *where* something happened.

Adverbial clauses of reason
Sometimes the subordinate clause will give a reason for the main clause. This is known as an **adverbial clause of reason**.

The match was cancelled because it was raining.

'. . . it was raining' was the *reason* for the match being cancelled.

As he was late home, they went out for a meal.

'. . . he was late home' is an adverbial clause of reason answering the question *why* they went out for a meal.

Adverbial clauses of manner
Like adverbs of manner, **adverbial clauses of manner** say *how* something is done.

She ran as though her life depended upon it.

The adverbial clause of manner 'her life depended on it' explains *how* she ran.

Adverbial clauses of comparison
An **adverbial clause of comparison** makes an explicit comparison.

Sandra works harder than her sister does.

Sandra is being compared with her sister.

Adverbial clauses of degree

An **adverbial clause of degree** will indicate the degree to which something is done.

I love you <u>more than I can say</u>.

He works <u>as hard as he can</u>.

Both the adverbial clauses of degree show to what extent 'I love' and 'he works'.

Adverbial clauses of purpose

Adverbial clauses of purpose indicate the *purpose* of the main clause.

The prisoner was locked in so that <u>he would not escape</u>.

The *purpose* of the locked door was to prevent the prisoner's escape.

Adverbial clauses of result

An **adverbial clause of result** shows what *results* from the main clause.

It was so hot that <u>her shirt was sticking to her</u>.

Her shirt was sticking to her as a *result* of the heat.

Adverbial clauses of condition

An adverbial clause of condition indicates the conditions under which something will be done.

<u>If</u> you finish your homework, <u>you may go out</u>.

Finishing the homework is the condition which must be fulfilled before the main clause 'you may go out' can take effect.

<u>Unless</u> it stops raining, <u>the repairs will not be completed</u>.

Including 'then'

If the subordinate clause begins with 'if', the main clause after the comma can sometimes begin with 'then'. In this case it does not need 'and' before it.

<u>If</u> fairy tales are entertainment, <u>*then* explaining the symbolism is a waste of time</u>.

The subjunctive

If the adverbial clause of condition suggests something that cannot be fulfilled, the **subjunctive** tense of the verb is used. The clause usually starts with 'if' and applies to the first or third persons. Instead of using 'was', 'were' is used.

If I <u>were</u> to tell you, you would not believe it.

If she <u>were</u> taller, she could be a model.

Relative pronouns

Relative pronouns have a similar function to conjunctions. They link subordinate clauses to main clauses. They are usually preceded by a noun.

The relative pronouns are:

which   that   who   whose   whom

'Which' and 'that' are linked to things while the others are used with people. 'That' can be either a conjunction or a relative pronoun. It depends how it is used.

I like the dress that is green.

'That' follows the noun 'dress' so it is a relative pronoun.

Notice that in the following examples the main clause has been 'split' by the subordinate clause which has been inserted into it. Commas have been placed either side of the subordinate clause.

The thief, who was a young boy, ran away.

The main clause is	The thief . . . ran away.
The subordinate clause is	. . . was a young boy

The subject of the subordinate clause is 'the thief' which is 'understood'.

The house, which had been empty for years, was now occupied.

Main clause:	The house . . . was now occupied.
Subordinate clause:	(The house) had been empty for years

The boy, whose trainers had been stolen, won the race.

Main clause:	The boy . . . won the race.
Subordinate clause:	. . . trainers had been stolen

The golfer, whom I supported, played very well.

Main clause:	The golfer . . . played very well.
Subordinate clause:	. . . I supported

The relative pronoun usually follows the noun to which it refers. This will avoid ambiguity. Make sure your writing is clear and that you have said what you mean. If your sentences are too long, it is easy for your reader to lose the sense of what you are saying.

Use of whom

'Whom' can sometimes be preceded by a preposition. There is a tendency today to ignore the traditional rule, 'Don't end a sentence with a preposition.' Prepositions are often found at the end of sentences today. However, those who wish to preserve the purity of the English language will probably keep the rule.

This is the boy <u>to whom</u> I gave the money.

The preposition, 'to' precedes 'whom'. The colloquial form would be:

This is the boy <u>who</u> I gave the money <u>to</u>.

In this case 'who' is used instead of 'whom' and the preposition 'to' ends the sentence. The 'who' could be omitted and 'understood'.

This is the boy I gave the money to.

Here are two more examples of the formal and the informal:

<u>To whom</u> are you speaking?

This sounds rather pompous so you would probably say:

<u>Who</u> are you speaking <u>to</u>?

It is the schoolmaster <u>for whom</u> the bell tolls.

It is the schoolmaster <u>who</u> the bells tolls <u>for</u>.

In the latter example the first sentence sounds better. Your choice of sentence will probably depend on the particular type of writing you are doing at the time.

Adjectival clauses

Like adjectives, the adjectival clause qualifies a noun or pronoun which is found in the main clause. Remember that *all* clauses *must* contain a subject (sometimes 'understood') and a finite verb.

He looked at the door which <u>was locked</u>.

The door is described as being locked. The adjectival clause is '. . . was locked'. The subject 'door' is 'understood' and the relative pronoun 'which' links the adjectival clause to the main clause. The finite verb in the adjectival phrase is 'was locked'.

His wife, <u>who is a model</u>, has gone on holiday.

'. . . is a model' describes the wife. The main clause is 'His wife . . . has gone on holiday'. The relative pronoun, 'who', links the adjectival clause to it. The finite verb in the adjectival clause is 'is'.

Adjectival clauses are often introduced by the following words:

who   whom   whose   which   that

'That' can sometimes be 'understood' so it is not always necessary to include it.

This is the house (that) they have built.

It is important to put the adjectival clause as close as possible to the noun or pronoun it is describing. If you don't, your sentence may be ambiguous.

She bought a dress from the charity shop which needed some repair.

Obviously it was the *dress* not the *shop* that needed repair!

She bought a dress, which needed some repair, from the charity shop.

CHECKLIST

◆ Each clause must contain a subject and a finite verb.

◆ There are main and subordinate clauses.

◆ Conjunctions and relative pronouns link clauses.

◆ A preposition shows the relation between one word and another.

◆ Don't use commas instead of full stops.

◆ A phrase is a group of words that does not contain a finite verb.

◆ There are different types of phrases.

◆ Adjectival clauses qualify a noun.

◆ There are a variety of adverbial clauses.

EXERCISES

1. Make each of the following groups of sentences into one sentence by using conjunctions or relative pronouns.

(a) Elaine was a popular teacher. She had worked at the same school for many years. She taught English.

(b) Clive was in a furious temper. His computer has crashed. He had to complete some work in a hurry.

(c) It was a beautiful day. The sun was shining. The birds

were singing. The flowers were smiling. Helen felt glad to be alive.

(d) The old lady put her hand on the shelf. It collapsed. She fell heavily bruising her face.

(e) The book launch was scheduled for October. It was postponed until November. The printer had not finished printing the books.

2. Pick out and name the clauses and phrases in the following sentences:

(a) Angrily, she flung the book on the table.

(b) The student wriggled his way into the pothole.

(c) He yearned to fly on Concorde.

(d) Dreaming of her holiday made her forget her unhappiness.

(e) Furiously angry, she shouted at her daughter.

(f) They have gone on holiday.

(g) To visit Australia was his ambition.

(h) The postponed match was to take place the following day.

(i) Gazing out of the window, he wondered what he should do next.

(j) Hurrying to catch her train, Denise tripped and fell heavily.

3. Pick out and identify the subordinate clauses in the following passage:

The prisoner, who had been badly beaten, crouched in the corner of his cell. He had been caught while he was climbing out of the window of the house where the terrorists had been hiding. He had gone there because a meeting had been arranged with the leader. If he had stayed in his hotel, he would have been safe. He had tried as hard as he could to persuade the terrorists to release their hostage but it had not worked. Unless something was done soon, the hostage would be killed.

4. Correct the following sentences:

(a) If I was a giant, I could reach that shelf.
(b) If she was to ask me, I would go.

See page 162 for suggested answers.

Sentence Variety

It is important to vary your sentence structure. If all your sentences are simple ones consisting of one main clause, the impression you give will be rather juvenile. You will need some simple sentences and you can vary their pattern but you will also need compound sentences (two or more main clauses) and complex sentences (a mixture of main clauses and subordinate clauses).

THE SIMPLE SENTENCE

As we have already seen, there are a number of variations you can use with the simple sentence. It does not always form the same pattern.

Examples

The simple sentence can consist of only two words.

Helen gasped.

This follows the accepted grammatical pattern. It has a subject (Helen) and a finite verb (gasped). The latter, as required, shows person (third), number (singular) and tense (past). The next sentence is slightly longer and contains an object as well.

She (subject) gripped (finite verb) the table (object).

It could be elaborated with the addition of a phrase.

She gripped the table <u>with both hands</u> (phrase).

Then, collapsing on the floor, she sobbed.

'Then' is an adverb of time introducing the participial phrase, 'collapsing on to the floor', which is followed by the main clause, 'she sobbed'.

The events of the day had upset her.

'The events of the day' is a noun phrase acting as the subject of the sentence.

'Had upset' is the finite verb.

'Her' is the object of the sentence.

She was terrified.

The above sentence uses the adjective 'terrified' as the complement of the sentence. It refers to the subject 'she'.

Never again would she go out alone.

This sentence starts with a phrase; the verb 'would' and the subject 'she' have been inverted in this construction. In the following sentence a phrase has been used as the complement.

It would cause more trouble.

'It' is the subject.

'Would cause' is the finite verb.

'More trouble' is a noun phrase used as the complement.

When all the sentences are put together, they make an acceptable paragraph. Although they are all simple sentences, the pattern has been varied to make the work more interesting.

> Helen gasped. She gripped the table with both hands. Then, collapsing on to the floor, she sobbed. The events of the day had upset her. She was terrified. Never again would she go out alone. It would cause more trouble.

COMPOUND SENTENCES

Compound sentences are composed of two or more main clauses and there are several variations that can be used. You can have a number of main clauses within one sentence provided your construction is correct. A clause has to contain a subject and a finite verb. You can have several clauses in a sentence and each of them will have a specific purpose. There are two types of clauses – main and subordinate. Each clause must contain a subject and a finite verb. Each sentence must contain at least one main clause. If there is only one clause in a sentence, it is a main clause and the sentence is a simple sentence. Remember that you *cannot* use a comma to separate two main clauses. Use a co-ordinating conjunction to join them or separate them using a full stop.

To join two main clauses to form a compound sentence, you will have to use one of the co-ordinating conjunctions, 'and', 'but', 'or'. The main clauses can consist of only a subject and a finite verb or they can be expanded with extra words or phrases.

(It was very quiet) and (there was a strange atmosphere).

The two bracketed main clauses are linked by the co-ordinating conjunction 'and'. The following sentence has three main clauses.

(She tried to get up) but (her legs were shaking) and (they would not support her).

The conjunction 'but' separates the first two main clauses. The final clause 'they would not support her' is introduced by 'and'. The pronoun 'they' could have been left out as it would have been 'understood'.

. . . her legs were shaking and would not support her.

The following sentence uses the conjunction 'or' to link the clauses.

(She must leave soon) or (it would be too dark to see).

> **Use a co-ordinating conjunction to link two clauses
> – *not* a comma.**

If your work is constructed properly, you can use a number of clauses within one sentence.

You can use a list of main clauses. In this case, as in any other list, the clauses are separated by commas and the last one is preceded by 'and'. Although it is not now considered necessary to put a comma before 'and', it is sometimes done. If so, it is known as the **Oxford comma** as the Oxford University Press uses it but many other publishers do not. If there is a danger of the sentence being misunderstood, then a comma should be inserted before 'and'. (Fowler, the acknowledged authority on English usage feels the omission of the **Oxford comma** is usually 'unwise'.) It is not used in the following examples. 'I' is the subject of each of the clauses in the following sentences but it needs to be used only once – at the beginning. It is 'understood' in the following clauses.

I closed down the computer, (I) signed my letters, (I) tidied my desk, (I) picked up my coat and (I) left the office.

It is certainly not necessary to include the 'I' in each clause. The first four main clauses are separated by commas and the last one is preceded by 'and'. In the following sentence the subject of each of the clauses is different so the subject obviously has to be included. Again, commas separate the first four and the last one is preceded by 'and'.

The wind howled round the house, the rain beat against the windows, the lightning flashed, the thunder roared and Sarah cowered under the table.

In the following sentence, although three of the clauses have the same subject 'he', the subject has to be included so the sentence makes sense.

He was annoyed, his wife was late, he disliked the house, he was very tired and the food was tasteless.

Because 'his wife was late' is between 'He was annoyed' and 'he disliked the house', 'he' has to be repeated.

THE COMMA

The comma was introduced into English in the sixteenth century and plays a very important part in punctuation. However, it must *not* be used instead of a full stop. If you write a sentence with two main clauses separated by a comma, it is *wrong*. Either put a full stop between them or use a conjunction to link them.

My name is Bob, I live in London.

This is wrong. It should be:

My name is Bob. I live in London.

or

My name is Bob and I live in London.

The two clauses could also be separated by a **semicolon**. There will be more about this later.

My name is Bob; I live in London.

Commas can be used for the following purposes:

◆ To separate items in a list. Remember there must be 'and' before the last one.

I went to the town and I bought some pens, a pencil, a file, a pad, a ruler and an eraser.

◆ To separate a list of main clauses.

Jack was doing his homework, his sister was practising the piano, their father was reading the paper and the baby was crying.

◆ To separate the subordinate clause from the main clause when starting the sentence with a subordinating conjunction.

Because she was ill, she stayed at home.

◆ To separate a subordinate clause in the middle of a main clause.

The dog, who was barking loudly, strained at his leash.

◆ After a participial phrase at the beginning of a sentence.

Looking out of the window, she realised it was raining.

◆ To separate phrases in the middle of a main clause.

The girl, tall and elegant, stepped into her car.

There will be more about commas in the chapter on dialogue.

COMPLEX SENTENCES

A complex sentence can contain any number of main clauses and subordinate clauses. It *must* contain at least *one* main clause and it must be carefully constructed so that all the clauses are linked correctly.

Subordinate clauses

There are a variety of subordinate clauses you can use to make your writing more interesting. Vary them and their positions so that your work 'flows'. Following are some examples:

She hobbled to the door which was shut.

Main clause:	She hobbled to the door . . .
Adjectival clause modifying the noun 'door':	. . . was shut.
Relative pronoun as link:	which

Before she could open it, she heard a noise.

Main clause:	. . . she heard a noise.
Adverbial clause of time:	. . . she could open it
Subordinating conjunction:	Before . . .

The comma separates the clauses because the sentence begins with a conjunction.

She ran to the window, which was open, and peered out.

Main clause:	She ran to the window . . .
Adjectival clause modifying 'window':	. . . was open . . .
Relative pronoun linking clauses:	. . . which . . .
Main clause (subject understood):	. . . (she) peered out.
Co-ordinating conjunction:	. . . and . . .

The man, who was looking up at her, looked very angry.

Main clause: The man . . .	. . . looked very angry.
Adjectival clause:	. . . was looking up at her . . .
Relative pronoun:	. . . who . . .

It was the man who had followed her and who had frightened her dog so he had run away.

Main clause:	It was the man . . .
Adjectival clause:	. . . had followed her . . .
Adjectival clause:	. . . had frightened her dog . . .
Adverbial clause of reason:	. . . he had run away.
Relative pronoun:	who
Subordinating conjunction:	so

Be careful with the construction in the above sentence. 'Who' has been used twice. You can only use 'and who' if it follows a subordinate clause which has been introduced by 'who'. In this sentence 'who followed her' is a subordinate clause introduced by 'who' so the 'and who' that follows later is correct. The following sentence is incorrect:

The man had followed her and who had frightened her dog.

The 'who' is, of course, unnecessary. It should be:

The man had followed her and had frightened her dog.

Shaking with fear, she rushed to the door and tried to open it while the doorbell rang persistently.

Main clause:	. . . she rushed to the door . . .
Main clause:	. . . tried to open it . . .
Co-ordinating conjunction:	. . . and . . .
Adverbial clause of time:	. . . the doorbell rang persistently
Participial phrase:	Shaking with fear . . .

She had to get away but the door was locked and she could not open it.

Main clause:	She had to get away . . .
Main clause:	. . . the door was locked . . .
Main clause:	. . . she could not open it.
Co-ordinating conjunctions:	. . . but . . . and . . .

While she was trying to open the door, a light appeared at the window and she screamed.

Main clause:	. . . a light appeared at the window . . .
Main clause:	. . . she screamed.
Adverbial clause of time:	. . . she was trying to open the door . . .

Subordinating conjunction: While . . .
Co-ordinating conjunction: . . . and . . .

Like the subjects of clauses, relative pronouns can also sometimes be omitted. They are 'understood' so the sense is not lost. Leaving out 'that' can often 'tighten' your writing.

I chose the book (that) you recommended.

Here is the article (that) I enjoyed.

'That' is unnecessary as both sentences can be understood without it.

I chose the book you recommended.

Here is the article I enjoyed.

There are occasions when properly constructed sentences are not used. When writing dialogue or using very informal language, the rules will sometimes be ignored although the words must still make sense.

Newspapers often omit words to make their headlines more eye-catching. Look at the following:

Murdered by her son
MP found guilty of fraud
Pile-up on the motorway
Miracle birth

All of these headlines make sense although words are missing from the 'sentences'. We also frequently ignore grammatical rules when we talk. We often use 'non-sentences' when writing notices.

A pound of apples please.
No smoking
Got a pencil?
What a nuisance!

All of these make sense although they are not proper sentences. They would not be used in formal writing.

In his amusing book, *The King's English*, Kingsley Amis describes the idea that you may not start a sentence with 'and' or 'but' as an 'empty superstition'. It *is* permissible to start a sentence or even a paragraph with either of the two co-ordinating conjunctions but they must not be overused in this way or they lose their effect. They can be used for emphasis or to suggest what is to follow later. But they must *not* be used as the continuation of the previous sentence. They should start a new idea but be used sparingly.

Examples using 'and'

He walked to the bus stop. And waited half an hour for a bus.

This is incorrect as the second sentence follows on from the first. No full stop is needed between the two clauses.

He walked to the bus stop and waited half an hour for a bus.

It was too cold and wet to go out. He was bored. And he had finished his library book.

The 'and' at the beginning of the last sentence adds momentum to the idea of the boredom. If the last two sentences were joined, it would not be as effective.

Examples using 'but'

'But' can be used in the same way. Remember not to use it at the beginning of a sentence if it is a continuation of the previous one.

She waited all day but her son did not come.

She waited all day. But her son did not come.

Either of the above examples would be acceptable although the second one has a stronger emphasis.

At last he met her again. But he had waited many years.

Joining these two sentences with 'but' would not work and some of the sense would be lost.

I hoped to play tennis but it rained all day.

This sentence is better using 'but' as a conjunction. Little would be gained if 'but' started a second sentence.

THE THREE MOODS

The mood refers to the particular attitude of the speaker or writer contained in the content of the sentence. There are three moods – the declarative mood, the interrogative mood and the imperative mood.

The declarative mood

The **declarative mood** is used when you are making a statement so this is the one you are likely to use most frequently. Properly constructed sentences will be used.

The man entered the house but found it empty. There was a chair overturned by the table and the window was open.

The interrogative mood

The **interrogative mood**, as its name suggests, is used for asking questions so is more likely to be used when you are writing dialogue.

'Is there anyone there?' he called. 'Where are you?'

It is also sometimes effective within a narrative to create a particular effect.

The imperative

The imperative is also more likely to be used in dialogue. It is used for commands.

Come here.
Put out that cigarette.
Stop talking.
Go to bed.

All of these are sentences and follow the rules but the subject, 'you' (second person – singular or plural) is understood. The person being given the orders is 'you'.

CHECKLIST

◆ Each sentence must contain at least one main clause.

◆ A simple sentence has only one main clause.

◆ A compound sentence contains two or more main clauses.

◆ A complex sentence contains a mixture of main and subordinate clauses.

◆ Don't use commas to separate two main clauses.

◆ Vary your sentence structure.

◆ There are a variety of different clauses you can use.

EXERCISES

1. Identify the phrases and clauses in the following sentences.

(a) The match was cancelled because of the weather.
(b) We can go when you are ready.
(c) The policeman chased the thief, caught him, handcuffed him and took him to the police station to charge him.
(d) Leaping out of the car, she dashed into the shop.
(e) Julie was doing her homework, Dan was laying the

table, their father was reading the paper and their mother was preparing dinner.

2. Punctuate the following passage:

George leapt out of bed stubbing his toe on the chair that was beside him hobbling to the window he stared gloomily out it was raining perhaps it would brighten up later he watched the milkman drive down the road he was late sleepily he drifted into the bathroom to wash and shave he cursed as he cut himself dabbing the blood with a piece of cotton wool he wondered how he would perform at the interview he must not be late

See page 164 for suggested answers.

4

Adjectives and Adverbs

The remaining parts of speech can be used to enhance your writing. **Adjectives** and **Adverbs** are **modifiers**. To modify means to add a word to another word to increase, lessen or change slightly its meaning.

ADJECTIVES

Adjectives are words which modify nouns or pronouns. A noun by itself can be very stark. It also does not always provide enough information. If you ask in a shop for oranges, you do not need to describe them but if you need help in buying a coat, you will have to give more information. Adjectives will be required to describe it:

blue   long   red   short   thick   thin

When writing, adjectives can add colour to your sentences and enable you to paint a picture with words. They are always related to a noun or pronoun and the most common ones are those which describe some quality in a person or thing.

Positioning your adjective

Adjectives can be placed before the noun, as in the following sentences:

She was wearing a <u>blue</u> dress.

They had a <u>delicious</u> meal.

The <u>clever</u> boy passed his exams.

If there is a list of adjectives before the noun, separate them with commas.

She was wearing a <u>blue, flowered</u> dress.

They had a <u>huge, delicious</u> meal.

The <u>clever, little</u> boy passed his exams.

You are a very <u>naughty, disobedient, mischievous</u> boy.

Adjectives can also be placed at the end of the sentence following the verb.

Her essay was <u>excellent</u>.

The sky grew <u>dark</u>.

The leaves turned <u>brown</u>.

If there is a list of adjectives at the end of the clause, remember that the last one must be preceded by 'and'.

The lecturer was handsome, kind, gentle and good-natured.

The book was readable, humorous and well-written.

COMPARISON OF ADJECTIVES

Adjectives can be used to compare one thing with another and to show varying degrees. Look at the following sentences.

Julie was <u>tall</u>.

Ben was <u>taller</u>.

Chris was the <u>tallest</u>.

In the first sentence 'tall' describes Julie. It is known as the **positive** degree. In the second one, 'taller' compares the two by implication and is known as the **comparative** degree. 'Tallest', the **superlative** degree, suggests that in the matter of height, Chris is superior to the other two.

To form the comparative for most adjectives 'er' is added while the superlative ends in 'est'.

Positive	Comparative	Superlative
bright	brighter	brightest
cold	colder	coldest
dark	darker	darkest
fast	faster	fastest
few	fewer	fewest
happy	happier	happiest
hot	hotter	hottest
nice	nicer	nicest
pale	paler	palest
pretty	prettier	prettiest
quick	quicker	quickest
sad	sadder	saddest
short	shorter	shortest
small	smaller	smallest
thick	thicker	thickest
thin	thinner	thinnest
wide	wider	widest

If the adjective ends in a single consonant, remember to double it before adding the ending.

If the adjective ends in 'y', remember to change it to an 'i' before adding 'er' or 'est'.

> **The comparative compares *two* things only. Use the superlative when more than two are involved.**

Exceptions

Not all adjectives follow the pattern illustrated above. Some words would be too clumsy to pronounce if 'er' or 'est' were added. In this case 'more' is added before the positive form for the comparative and 'most' for the superlative.

Positive	Comparative	Superlative
beautiful	more beautiful	most beautiful
benevolent	more benevolent	most benevolent
careful	more careful	most careful
energetic	more energetic	most energetic
evil	more evil	most evil
rapid	more rapid	most rapid

Sometimes the superlative is used for emphasis rather than comparison.

It was <u>most</u> kind of you to invite me.

He is <u>most</u> particular about the creases in his trousers.

The child is <u>most</u> careful when she crosses the road.

With some comparatives and superlatives you have a choice. You can add 'er' and 'est' *or* 'more' and 'most'. Do *not* use both!

lovely	lovelier (more lovely)	loveliest (most lovely)
clever	cleverer (more clever)	cleverest (most clever)

This rule has *no* exceptions. You either use one or the other.

Do *not* use more lovelier or most cleverest!

Some adjectives change the word for the comparative and superlative.

Postive	*Comparative*	*Superlative*
bad	worse	worst
far	farther (*or* further)	farthest (*or* furthest)
good	better	best
little	less	least
much	more	most

Some adjectives because of their meaning stand alone and the comparative and superlative forms cannot be used. Some of these are:

    perfect   round   square   unique   excellent

Possessive adjectives

Don't confuse **possessive adjectives** with possessive pronouns which usually stand alone. Possessive adjectives usually precede a noun. They are:

    my   your   his   her   its   our   their

That is <u>my</u> book.

Where is <u>your</u> homework?

<u>His</u> behaviour was atrocious.

<u>Her</u> hair looks pretty.

<u>Its</u> fur was wet

This is <u>our</u> house.

<u>Their</u> daughters are visiting today.

Personal Pronoun	Possessive Pronoun	Possessive Adjective
I	mine	my
you	yours	your
he	his	his
she	hers	her
it	its	its
we	ours	our
they	theirs	their

None of the possessive pronouns have apostrophes.

The possessive adjective should also be used before a gerund (verbal noun) as in the following examples:

I hope you don't mind <u>my</u> mentioning it.

'Mentioning' is the gerund and 'my' the possessive adjective that modifies it.

His parents disapproved of <u>his</u> smoking.

'Smoking' is the gerund and 'his' the possessive adjective that modifies it.

Note that the *object* form is incorrect. The following sentences are wrong.

I hope you don't mind <u>me</u> mentioning it.

His parents disapproved of <u>him</u> smoking.

'Me' and 'him' are objects and cannot serve as adjectives.

Demonstrative adjectives

Demonstrative adjectives are the same words as demonstrative pronouns but they are always used *before* a noun, not alone. They are:

    this   that   these   those

<u>This</u> book is very readable.

<u>That</u> pavilion has just been built.

<u>These</u> apples are very juicy.

<u>Those</u> flowers are beautiful.

'This' (singular) and 'these' (plural) are used for something nearby. 'That' (singular) and 'Those' (plural) are used for things at a distance.

Interrogative adjectives

Interrogative adjectives, which also precede a noun, are used to ask questions and a question mark is placed at the end.

<u>Whose</u> book is this?

<u>Which</u> coat do you prefer?

<u>What</u> town is this?

When are you going away?

Why have you told me?

Adjectives showing quantity

Some adjectives can indicate the number or quantity. They must precede a noun.

There were few people present.

There were only ten players on their team.

There were many phone calls as a result of the advertisement.

She won several matches.

They showed no interest in the house.

Have you any money?

There are some biscuits left in the tin.

'Few' is a strange word as it can be used in different ways.

I intend to take a few days off.

This indicates the number of days but not when and uses the indefinite article 'a'.

There are few telephones left in the sale.

This suggests there are hardly any telephones left and no article is used.

The few days remaining she spent clearing her desk.

This indicates the particular days that are left and uses the definite article 'the'.

Noun used as an adjective

Sometimes a noun is used as an adjective. You can tell which part of speech it is because of its function in the sentence.

He climbed over the <u>garden</u> wall.

'Garden' is an adjective modifying wall.

She walked into the <u>garden</u>.

'Garden' is a noun.

I received twenty <u>birthday</u> cards.

'Birthday' is an adjective modifying 'cards'.

It was my <u>birthday</u> yesterday.

'Birthday' is a noun.

They chose <u>apple</u> pie for dessert.

'Apple' is an adjective modifying 'pie'.

Most of the <u>apples</u> fell off the tree.

'Apples' is a noun.

They wore <u>summer</u> dresses for the outing.

'Summer' is an adjective modifying 'dresses'.

She bought new dresses for the <u>summer</u>.

'Summer' is a noun.

The girls disliked their <u>school</u> uniform.

'School' is an adjective modifying 'uniform'.

Their <u>school</u> was burgled last week.

'School' is a noun.

The present participle used as an adjective

The present participle which ends in 'ing' can also be used as an adjective if it is placed before a noun to describe it.

The mother picked up the <u>crying</u> baby.

The child was frightened of the <u>barking</u> dog.

The plumber mended the <u>dripping</u> tap.

She stared sadly at the <u>pouring</u> rain.

Capital letters

When forming an adjective from a proper noun *always* start with a capital letter.

Proper Noun	Adjective
Belgium	Belgian
England	English
France	French
Spain	Spanish

> **All adjectives relating to countries begin with a capital letter.**

Dutch	Flemish

Adjectives should be used sparingly. Don't litter your work with them. Use them to enhance your writing. Never use them to 'pad' your work. Some adjectives are grossly over-worked. 'Nice', 'good', and 'bad' are examples. Find synonyms (similar words) to replace them. If you can't think of one use a thesaurus to help you. There will be more about the thesaurus later.

ADVERBS

Adverbs are words that qualify or modify verbs, adjectives or other adverbs. There are various types.

Adverbs of manner

Adverbs of manner usually end in 'ly'. They say *how* something is done. They are formed by adding 'ly' to an adjective and they contribute to the meaning of the verb. The following list gives you some examples.

Adjective	Adverb
beautiful	beautifully
brisk	briskly
careful	carefully

cold	coldly
comfortable	comfortably
immediate	immediately
pretty	prettily
quick	quickly
slow	slowly
stealthy	stealthily

He <u>walked</u> quickly down the lane.

She writes <u>beautifully</u>.

<u>Unsteadily</u> she stood up.

If the adjective ends in 'l', you must still add 'ly' so there will be a double 'l' at the end: beautiful – beautifully.

For adjectives that end in 'le' change the 'e' to a 'y': comfortable   comfortably

For adjectives that end in a consonant followed by 'e', simply add 'ly': immediate   immediately

> **Do *not* change the position of the 'e' to make the ending 'ley'!**

COMPARISON OF ADVERBS

Adverbs of manner can be compared in the same way as adjectives. As most of them end in 'ly' the comparative will usually have 'more' in front of it and the superlative will have 'most' in front of it.

Positive	*Comparative*	*Superlative*
beautifully	more beautifully	most beautifully
brightly	more brightly	most brightly
carefully	more carefully	most carefully

Exceptions:

badly	worse	worst
little	less	least
much	more	most
well	better	best

As with the adjectives, the superlative can also be used for emphasis.

He drove <u>most</u> carefully.

The embroidery was done <u>most</u> skilfully.

Adverbs can be placed at the beginning of a sentence, in the middle or at the end.

<u>Carefully</u>, he placed the box on the table.

He placed the box <u>carefully</u> on the table.

He placed the box on the table <u>carefully</u>.

The last one is not as good as the other two. The placing of the adverb will depend on the sentence.

'Hopefully' is often used incorrectly to replace the verb.

<u>Hopefully</u> I shall pass my exams.

This should be:

I hope I shall pass my exams.

or

It is hoped I shall pass my exams.

'Hopefully' is an adverb which should be used to modify a verb.

The dog dug <u>hopefully</u> for the bone.

'Regretfully' and 'thankfully' are also used incorrectly.

<u>Regretfully</u> we shall not be able to attend your wedding.

This should be:

<u>We regret</u> we shall not be able to attend your wedding.

or

<u>It is regretted</u> that we shall not be able to attend your wedding.

<u>Thankfully</u> we reached the shore before the storm broke.

This should be:

<u>We were thankful</u> that we reached the shore before the storm broke.

Exceptions

The following words end in 'ly' but they are adjectives:

    friendly   kindly   leisurely   lonely   lovely

To make them into adverbs you should change the 'y' to an 'i' and then add 'ly'.

    friendlily   kindlily   leisurelily   lonelily   lovelily

The words are rather clumsy so they are rarely used and today the adjective is often accepted as an adverb as well. It is better to use another word or change your sentence so you can use the adjective. Instead of:

    The nurse behaved <u>kindlily</u> to the patient.

It would be better to say:

    The nurse behaved in a <u>kindly manner</u> towards the patient.

Here are two more examples;

    She walked <u>leisurelily</u> through the woods.

    She took a <u>leisurely walk</u> through the woods.

    He gestured <u>friendlily</u> to his partner.

    He made a <u>friendly gesture</u> towards his partner.

When adjectives ending in 'ic' are made into adverbs, 'ally' is added instead of just 'ly'.

    ecstatic   ecstatically   enthusiastic   enthusiastically

Adverbs of time

Adverbs of time say *when* something takes place. Look at the following examples. The adverbs of time are underlined.

Robert went to London <u>yesterday</u>.

She arrived <u>late</u> for her interview.

The party is <u>tomorrow</u>.

The train will <u>soon</u> be here.

<u>Then</u> they entered the castle.

The match has <u>now</u> ended.

Then is an adverb of time. Do *not* use it as a conjunction to join clauses! If you place it between two clauses put **and** before it.

They locked the car and then went to the town.

not: They locked the car, then went to the town.

Adverbs of place

Adverbs of place say *where* something took place. All the following sentences answer the question 'where?' The adverbs of place are underlined.

The fog swirled <u>around</u>.

The play will take place <u>there</u>.

<u>Here</u> is your packed lunch.

We went <u>abroad</u> this year.

The golf player searched <u>everywhere</u> for his ball.

Interrogative adverbs

Interrogative adverbs ask a question and usually start the sentence. They answer the questions: where? how? why? when?

Where are you going?

How are you?

Why did you buy it?

When do you go on holiday?

> **Don't forget to put a question mark at the end!**

Some of the words used as adverbs can also be used as other parts of speech depending on their use in the sentence.

Adverbs of number and degree

Adverbs of number show how often an action takes place.

He scored twice.

The child was allowed to go on the roundabout once.

Adverbs of degree show the extent to which an action takes place.

I quite like it.

The area had been completely devastated by the bomb.

You have had enough.

Adverbs of degree can also modify adjectives and other adverbs.

In the following examples all the adverbs modify the adjective they precede.

It was <u>extremely</u> hot.

The adverb 'extremely' modifies the adjective 'hot'.

He was <u>very</u> kind.

The adverb 'very' modifies the adjective 'kind'.

She was <u>terribly</u> upset.

The adverb 'terribly' modifies the adjective 'upset'.

He was <u>too</u> late for the wedding.

The adverb 'too' modifies the adjective 'late'.

In the following examples the adverbs modify other adverbs.

Joan has worked <u>fairly</u> hard.

The adverb 'fairly' modifies the adverb 'hard'.

The winner ran <u>exceedingly</u> fast.

The adverb 'exceedingly' modifies the adverb 'fast'.

Some adverbs cannot be classified in the same way as those above. Words like 'yes', 'no' and 'not' are sometimes classified as adverbs. So are words that suggest agreement or uncertainty as in the following.

assuredly	certainly	maybe	perhaps
probably	surely		

<u>Certainly</u> you can come with me.

<u>Surely</u> it's going to be fine.

It's <u>probably</u> going to rain.

'Maybe' and 'perhaps' have similar meanings. 'Perhaps' is the more formal word. 'Maybe' can be used when writing in a more colloquial style or in dialogue.

As with adjectives, some adverbs are used unnecessarily. By their incessant use, they often lose their impact and even their meaning can become obscured. Look at the following examples.

He's a <u>terrifyingly</u> good player.

'Terrifyingly' has connotations of terror but this sentence debases the word. Why not replace both adverb and adjective with 'excellent'?

He's an <u>excellent</u> player.

What about the following?

She cooked a <u>superbly</u> delicious meal.

This is going 'over the top'. Use the adjective 'superb' by itself.

She cooked a <u>superb</u> meal.

The following are familiar expressions but in all of them the adverb has lost its original meaning.

I'm <u>frightfully</u> sorry.

She's <u>awfully</u> happy.

He's <u>terribly</u> kind.

The word 'only' should be placed immediately *before* the word or phrase it is intended to modify.

He <u>only</u> went to the Tower of London. (He went nowhere else.)

Jeff is the <u>only</u> one allowed to visit her. (No one else can go.)

She spoke <u>only</u> to her friends. (She spoke to no one else.)

Other words that follow a similar pattern are:

| even | mainly | often | quite | rarely |

It is <u>quite</u> ready.

Her garden is <u>mainly</u> grass.

She could not <u>even</u> write her name.

They <u>rarely</u> go out.

It <u>often</u> rains in August.

Other Adverbs

Adverbs can also be used to modify or help other adverbs:

The ambulance came <u>very</u> quickly.

The adverb 'very' modifies the other adverb 'quickly'.

Adverbs can also be used with adjectives to modify them.

I am extremely <u>well</u>, thank you.

The adverb 'extremely' modifies the adjective 'well'.

Other adverbs used in this way are: too, much, more, however.

CHECKLIST

◆ Adjectives qualify or modify nouns or pronouns.

◆ Adjectives formed from a proper noun start with a capital letter.

◆ Don't confuse possessive pronouns and possessive adjectives.

◆ Adverbs qualify or modify verbs, adjectives and other adverbs.

EXERCISES

1. Pick out the adjectives from the following passage.

It was a beautiful day; there was no sign of rain so Doreen and Jack decided to go for a long walk along the cliff top. Having sauntered along for two hours, they stopped at a picturesque pub for a welcome coffee and some biscuits. Their feet were very sore and they were glad to sit in the attractive garden on the wooden benches overlooking the small bay. The only sound was the distant roaring of the sea and the crying of the gulls. It was so peaceful.

2. Identify the types of adverbs in the following passage.

Doreen looked dreamily over the bay. Jack was taking a leisurely stroll to the cliff edge and she watched him lazily. Carefully, she eased her feet out of her shoes and leant back, sighing happily. She knew they would be too late for tea if they did not soon move but she felt so content. Butterflies floated around and she wondered why anyone ever went abroad. Why not stay in this very beautiful country? It had so much to offer.

See page 165 for suggested answers.

Claire passed the test with flying colours; Laura failed.

'Laura failed' stands in stark contrast to the previous sentence.

There is no reason why complex sentences should not also use semicolons.

Because it was raining, they stayed indoors; they played Scrabble.

The first section contains a subordinate clause followed by a main clause. The second one contains only a main clause.

Using a semicolon can provide variety in your writing. You have a range of possible sentence patterns. Vary the length of your sentences. Don't make them too long. A simple sentence can be effective if it follows a series of complex ones. Sometimes a number of short sentences can be used to build up suspense in a story. If you use complex sentences, make sure they are constructed correctly.

You can also use a semicolon to separate a list of items when these contain commas. In this case clauses are not used.

Those present at the conference were the Chairman of the Governors, Mr Ken Regan; the Headmistress, Ms Judith Ray; the Deputy, Mr John Smith; two members of staff, Mrs Kay Winter and Mr Tom King.

Commas only, could have been used provided the last one was preceded by 'and'. However, as each name is rather long, it is better to break up the sentence with semi-colons.

THE COLON

The **colon** was adopted into the English language in the sixteenth century. It is not one of the most frequently used punctuation marks. Like the semicolon, it is not followed by a capital letter. It has several purposes.

◆ To introduce examples expanding the previous sentence.

It had not rained for months: the ground was dry, the animals were dying and there was nothing to harvest.

◆ To introduce a list.

The following items were put into the auction: a Victorian gilt mirror, a Constable painting, an Edwardian chair and a tapestry needlecase.

◆ To emphasise two main clauses.

To err is human: to forgive, divine (the finite verb 'is' is understood).

◆ To reinforce the previous sentence.

I have no sense of direction: I always get lost when I visit a new town.

THE DASH

The **dash** is often overworked today. If it is used too much, it loses its effect. Use it sparingly and *never* use it instead of a comma or full stop. It can be used for emphasis but not too frequently.

Use it in the middle of a sentence to separate your additional words: a dash should go either side of them.

> I saw – or thought I saw – a white figure disappearing into the woods.

A single dash can be used between two clauses to reinforce the first one.

> Your spelling is weak – you must learn the basic rules.

BRACKETS

Round brackets can sometimes be used instead of dashes to insert an extra idea into a sentence. Like dashes, they should be used sparingly.

> The Millennium Dome (in spite of all the problems) was completed on time.

Both dashes and brackets can usually be replaced by commas if they are in the middle of a sentence.

> I saw, or thought I saw, a white figure disappearing into the woods.

> The Millennium Dome, in spite of all the problems, was completed on time.

Square brackets are used when words within a quotation are not part of the original material.

> The lecturer stated, 'I consider this play [Hamlet] to be Shakespeare's greatest.'

Extra ideas that are inserted in this way to expand the sentence are known as **parentheses**. If said aloud, they are spoken in a lower tone and there is a pause either side of them. They resemble 'throwaway' lines.

Do not use parentheses too frequently or they will lose their impact. They will interrupt the 'flow' of your work and irritate your reader. Used sparingly, they are effective but usually it is better to rework them into the main structure of your sentence. Think carefully before you use them and make sure they are used correctly and add something to your sentence.

THE QUESTION MARK

A **question mark** is *always* placed at the end of a question. *Do* remember it. So many people forget to include it. If you have used a question mark, you do *not* require a full stop as well.

> Where are you?
>
> It's not raining, is it?

If you are reporting a question that someone else has said, you do not need a question mark.

She asked if I had change for a pound.

However, if the actual question she asked is used, a question mark *is* required.

'Do you have change for a pound?' she asked.

Notice that the question mark goes *inside* the inverted commas. There will be more about dialogue in Chapter 7.

Single words that ask a question are also followed by a question mark.

How?   Why?   When?   Where?   Who?   What?

THE EXCLAMATION MARK

Like the dash, the **exclamation mark** should be used rarely if it is not to lose its effect. Do *not* use it for emphasis. Your choice of words should convey this. If a speaker exclaims, an exclamation mark should be used after the words.

'Don't touch me!' she exclaimed.

The word 'exclaimed' does not have to be used. It can be suggested, as in the following sentence:

'They've won!' she shouted.

An exclamation mark can also be used to indicate an element of irony. The speaker or writer is commenting with 'tongue in cheek'.

He was given a new bike for Christmas. Now he's set to win the Olympics!

You must *not* use a full stop as well as an exclamation mark. Neither is it correct to use several exclamation marks for emphasis. Use them rarely or they will lose their effect.

CHECKLIST

◆ A semicolon can separate main clauses.
◆ Do not use a comma instead of a semicolon or full stop.
◆ Do not use a capital letter after a semicolon or a colon.
◆ Don't forget the question mark after a question.
◆ Don't overuse the exclamation mark.

EXERCISES

Punctuate the following passage:

David flung open the office door and sat down at his desk he had a great deal to do would he complete the report in time he knew he should not have left it till the last moment switching on the computer he keyed in the password and started to list the items to be included the statement from the assessors the secretary's report the year's accounts and the government recommendations crash he started what was that rushing to the window he looked out two men or was it more were running across the road.

See page 166 for suggested answers.

Apostrophes and Abbreviations

Apostrophes have two purposes. They can be used to show possession or to indicate the omission of a letter or letters.

POSSESSION

When a noun has something belonging to it, an apostrophe is placed at the end of the word and the 'possession' follows. When a singular noun shows possession, the apostrophe is put at the end of the word and an 's' is added.

The horse's coat shone.

Clive's cricket ball broke the window.

The dog tore the child's coat.

> **The apostrophe comes *before* the 's' when singular.**

If there is already an 's' at the end of the word, the rule still applies. Some words end in double 's'.

The princess's gown was the most beautiful at the ball.

The witness's evidence was false.

In some cases, particularly in names, the extra 's' can be omitted when there is a single 's' at the end of the word.

His Achilles' tendon was torn.

His father mended James' toy engine.

Some of Dickens' novels have been televised.

To make a noun plural, you usually have to add an 's'. Because the 's' is already there, you do not need to add one when putting in the apostrophe. Put the apostrophe *after* the 's'.

The ladies' cloakroom was closed for renovation.

The boys' playground was flooded.

> **Put the apostrophe *after* the 's' when plural**.

Don't forget to add 'es' if the word ends in double 's'.

The duchesses' hats were spectacular.

The waitresses' aprons were dirty.

> **Do *not* use an apostrophe merely because the noun is plural; for example, 'potatoes' for sale' is incorrect**.

There are a number of words which do *not* add an 's' for the plural. In some cases the word is changed.

Singular	*Plural*
child	children
foot	feet
goose	geese
man	men
mouse	mice
tooth	teeth
woman	women

Words that do *not* end in 's' to make the plural are treated the same as singular nouns when they are made possessive. The apostrophe follows the word and an 's' is added.

> The children's adventure playground proved very popular.

> The mice's tails looked like rubber tubes.

> The men's golf tournament was cancelled.

> The women's lunch was held at a luxurious hotel.

If there are two nouns indicating ownership of one thing, the apostrophe will be placed after the second noun.

> Chris and Daniel's boat is moored at Bosham.

Apostrophes are also needed in the following examples:

> She was given a week's notice.

> They had two months' holiday.

ABBREVIATIONS

When writing in a formal style, do not abbreviate words unless you are using dialogue.

If you omit letters from a word to abbreviate it, put an apostrophe in place of the letters.

Cannot	Can't
Could have	Could've
Do not	Don't
It has	It's
It is	It's

> 'Its' possessive has *no* apostrophe.
> It's = it is or it has
> The abbreviation for 'have' is 've' *not* 'of'.
> Could've = could have   Might've = might have

If a word is shortened and therefore the missing letters are at the *end* of the word, a full stop is used to indicate this:

abbreviation	abbr.
adjective	adj.
adverb	adv.
document	doc.
etcetera	etc.
information	info.
language	lang.

The names of counties are also shortened and require full stops. They always start with capital letters.

Berkshire	Berks.
Buckinghamshire	Bucks.
Gloucestershire	Glos.
Lincolnshire	Lincs.
Nottinghamshire	Notts.
Staffordshire	Staffs.

Counties that have their own abbreviations also require full stops.

| Hampshire | Hants. |
| Oxfordshire | Oxon. |

If you write the initials of a person's name before the surname, separate them with a full stop.

| B.J. Brown | M.R. Moss | V.A. Thomas |

However, it is becoming increasingly common to omit the full stop particularly when typing the name.

Titles can be abbreviated if they are followed by the person's *full* name and a full stop is then used. The abbreviation should *not* be used if only the surname follows it.

Capt. Kenneth Smythe or Captain Smythe *not* Capt. Smythe

Prof. Ian Blythe or Professor Blythe *not* Prof. Blythe

Rev. Anthony Harris or Reverend Harris *not* Rev. Harris

CONTRACTIONS

Contractions are when the abbreviation is created by using the first and last letters of the original word. A full stop at the end is *not* required.

Doctor	Dr	Mister	Mr
Mistress	Mrs	Road	Rd
Saint	St	Street	St

No full stop is required after a contraction.

INITIAL LETTERS

The names of many groups and organisations are now better known by the initial letters of their names. No full stop between the letters is required.

BA	Bachelor of Arts
BBC	British Broadcasting Corporation
BC	Before Christ
MP	Member of Parliament
RAF	Royal Air Force
USA	United States of America

ACRONYMS

Other initial letters can be pronounced as words. These are known as **acronyms**. It is becoming so common to use acronyms that we often forget what the letters stand for. No full stops are needed between the letters. Here are some examples:

AIDS	Acquired Immune Deficiency Syndrome
ASH	Action on Smoking and Health
LAMDA	London Academy of Music and Dramatic Art
NATO	North Atlantic Treaty Organisation
RADA	Royal Academy of Dramatic Art
UNICEF	United Nations Children's Emergency Fund
VAT	Value Added Tax

CHECKLIST

◆ An apostrophe is used to show possession or when letters are omitted.

◆ The apostrophe goes *before* the 's' when the noun is singular.

♦ The apostrophe goes *after* the 's' when the noun is plural.

♦ Do not use full stops after contractions.

♦ An acronym is a word formed from the initial letters of other words.

EXERCISES

Put apostrophes where necessary in the following passage. You may have to correct some words.

Johns parents were going on a weeks holiday. While they were away, he would stay at his grandparents house. He hoped theyd take him to the childrens adventure playground. He would go on lots of rides. His mothers dog would be put in the kennels while they were away. His friends family was going on a months holiday to America. John had been very envious of Bens new suitcase.

His parents and Bens parents took the two boys out for a meal before they left. John noticed that the waitress stockings were laddered. He didnt like some of the food on the menu but eventually decided on the 'chefs special'. He would of liked a hamburger but it was not available.

See page 166 for suggested answers.

Dialogue

Within a short story, a novel or even a biography, dialogue can be written either as direct speech or as indirect speech.

DIRECT SPEECH

Direct speech is the actual words that are said by a character. They are enclosed in inverted commas and there are rules to be followed:

◆ When a person starts to speak, always begin a new paragraph.

◆ The paragraph begins at the beginning of the sentence in which the speech occurs.

◆ The first word of a person's speech always starts with a capital letter.

◆ Always put a punctuation mark before closing the inverted commas.

◆ A comma is usually used to separate the speech from words before or after it.

◆ Use a full stop if no words follow the speech.

◆ The punctuation mark always goes *inside* the inverted commas.

Examples

'I don't want to go,' she said.

He replied, 'It is important.'

Notice the commas before 'she' and after 'replied' and the full stop after 'important'. If a question is asked, a question mark replaces the comma. You do *not* need both punctuation marks.

'Are you going to London?' she asked.

> There must *always* be a punctuation mark before the inverted commas are closed.

Sometimes the sentence is broken in the middle by 'she said' or something similar. In this case the punctuation is a little more complicated. If the speech is broken in the middle of a sentence, a comma follows the extra words.

'I know,' Esther remarked, 'where the treasure is hidden.'

There is a comma after 'remarked' because Esther has not completed her sentence. However, if the sentence is completed but the speaker continues to speak, a full stop is needed.

'I know where the treasure is hidden,' remarked Esther. 'It's beneath the apple tree in Bingham's Wood.'

Here, two separate sentences have been interrupted by 'remarked Esther'. The full stop could not have been placed after 'hidden' so it comes after 'Esther'. If a speaker speaks for several sentences, close the inverted commas at the end of the speech. Do not close them at the end of each sentence.

Commas are also used when someone is addressed by name. Depending on the position of it, the comma goes before or after the name.

'John, come here,' said the teacher.

'Come here, John,' said the teacher.

A comma is also used before the following phrases at the end of a sentence:

didn't you? won't it? hasn't he? don't you? didn't she? etc.

It won't rain, will it?

She hasn't got a coat, has she?

Sometimes this type of question is **rhetorical**. That means it does not require an answer.

Duologue

If there are only two speakers, it is not always necessary to identify them after each speech. Each person's speech is one paragraph even if it is only a single word. When the speech is finished, start a new paragraph when you return to the narrative.

'Laura's coming to dinner,' announced Helen.

'Why did you invite her?' demanded her husband. 'You know I can't stand her.'

'She took me out for lunch so I wanted to repay her invitation. You don't really mind, do you?'

'Is anyone else coming?'

'No.'

'I think I'll go to the pub,' remarked Jerry. 'Two's company. Three's a crowd.'

'Oh please, Jerry,' pleaded Helen, 'don't go. She'll think it so strange.'

'Too bad.'

'Don't be late, will you?'

He headed for the door and slammed it behind him. Helen burst into tears.

Paragraphs

If, for some reason, a character is speaking for a long time, the words will have to be broken up into paragraphs. Perhaps a story is being told. It might continue for several pages. In this case put inverted commas at the *beginning* of each paragraph but do not close them until the person has finished speaking.

Quotations

Occasionally a quotation may be incorporated within the direct speech. This will also need inverted commas to separate it from the main body of the speech. You can use either single or double inverted commas to enclose direct speech. If you have used single ones, use double ones for your quotation or vice versa. If the quotation comes at the end of the speech, put the punctuation mark *after* the 'quotation marks' and then close the inverted commas.

Harry asked, 'Who said, "Greater love has no man than this that a man lay down his life for his friends"?'

Harry is asking a question so the question mark goes *after* the quotation and *then* the inverted commas are closed.

TITLES

You will also need inverted commas when writing the titles of books, plays, films, etc. (If you are typing, put the titles in italics and do not use inverted commas.)

Shakespeare's play 'Hamlet' is one of the greatest plays ever written.

If a title is used within direct speech, the same rules apply as for quotations.

'I'm going to see the film "Shakespeare in Love",' announced Julie.

"For GCSE we're studying 'Romeo and Juliet', 'Far from the Madding Crowd' and 'Anthology of War Poems'," Peter told his mother.

Notice that each title is enclosed in inverted commas. In the first example single inverted commas have been used for the direct speech and double for the title. In the second example it is the other way round. Nowadays publishers usually use single inverted commas for direct speech.

INDIRECT SPEECH

Sometimes you may wish to 'report' what someone has said rather than quote the actual words. This is called **indirect speech** or 'reported speech' and no inverted commas are needed. In the following example the direct speech has been changed to indirect.

Direct speech: 'I am going to London,' she said.

Indirect speech: She said that she was going to London.

The conjunction 'that' has been added and the first person 'I' has been changed to the third person 'she'. All pronouns and possessive adjectives must also be changed into the third person when writing indirect speech. The tense has been changed from the present to the past.

In all cases of indirect speech there must be a 'saying' verb followed by 'that'. (Sometimes 'that' can be omitted and 'understood'.) The tense of the 'saying' verb determines the tense of the verbs that follow it. In the previous example 'said' is the past tense so the past tense is used in 'was going' and 'said'. Look at the following examples:

Ben Williams <u>reports</u> from Brussels that the European Parliament <u>is</u> now sitting.

The government <u>announced</u> that the crisis <u>was</u> over.

The sales force <u>reports</u> that business <u>is</u> booming.

Because indirect speech is not so 'immediate' as direct speech, some words also need to be changed:

here	becomes	there
this	becomes	that
these	becomes	those
today	becomes	that day
tomorrow	becomes	the following day
yesterday	becomes	the previous day

'I've been <u>here</u> before,' he said.

He said that he had been <u>there</u> before.

'Did you go out <u>yesterday</u>, Sally?' asked John.

John asked Sally if she had gone out <u>the previous day</u>.

'We'll go to the Zoo <u>tomorrow</u>,' he told his son.

He told his son (that) they would go to the Zoo <u>the following day</u>.

The word 'that' could be omitted so it is 'understood'; 'he told his son' has been moved to the beginning of the sentence.

WRITING A PLAY

Inverted commas are not required when writing a play. Stage directions are shown in italics or brackets. The characters' names are followed by a colon. When one character leaves the stage, the stage direction is 'Exit'. When two or more characters leave the stage, use the plural form 'Exeunt'.

(Enter Helen and David. He is carrying a tray of tea.)

Helen: Put the tray on the table, please.

David: (Puts tray on table) Do you want me to pour?

Helen: No, it's all right. I'll wait till Betty comes in.

David: Shall I call her?

Helen: No thank you. She said she had to finish a letter. She'll be here soon.

CHECKLIST

◆ Direct speech is enclosed in inverted commas.

◆ Always put a punctuation mark before closing the inverted commas.

◆ A new paragraph is used for each speaker.

◆ No inverted commas are used for indirect speech.

◆ Put a colon after the character when writing a play and do not use inverted commas.

EXERCISES

1. Correct the following passage:

Alan stared at his wife in dismay are you sure your pregnant he asked of course Im sure she replied crossly

but we agreed we couldnt afford a baby yet did you forget
to take the pill I suppose I must have done what are we
going to do about it he queried there's nothing we can do
of course there is I wont have an abortion if thats what
you mean I might of agreed once but not now but how can
we afford to keep a child he said in exasperation we hardly
afford to keep ourselves dont be so ridiculous Kate scoffed
Im going to read the pamphlet the doctor gave me its
called Baby Care she left the room before he could reply.

2. Set out the above passage in play form.

See page 167 for suggested answers.

Common Mistakes

It is important always to check your work to make sure you have not made any careless mistakes.

PUNCTUATION

Always check that your punctuation is correct. Make sure you have not used commas instead of full stops. If you are in doubt, always use a full stop or a semicolon. If you do this, you are less likely to make a mistake. Remember that each sentence must contain at least one main clause. A main clause consists of the subject and a finite verb. There may be additional words but they are optional. Don't forget to put a question mark at the end of a question.

AGREEMENT OF NOUNS AND VERBS

If a noun is singular, it must be followed by the singular form of the verb. Remember that collective nouns are singular although they refer to a number of people or objects. It is a common mistake to use the plural form of the verb with some collective nouns. 'Government' is a *singular* noun so the singular form of the verb should be used with it.

The government <u>is</u> planning to hold a referendum.

The team <u>was</u> playing very well.

The following words are also singular:

each   everyone   everything   nobody   someone

Everyone <u>is</u> here.

Each of you <u>has</u> three questions to answer.

Everything <u>is</u> ready.

<u>Has</u> nobody come?

Someone <u>has</u> done this.

'Either . . . or' and 'neither . . . nor' are also followed by the singular form of the verb if the nouns are singular.

Either you or your partner <u>was</u> given the manuscript.

Neither Jane nor Peter <u>was</u> allowed to go on the trip.

However if the nouns are plural, the plural form will be used.

Neither his employers nor his colleagues <u>are</u> willing to support him.

If two nouns are used before a verb, the following verb will be plural.

Jack and Mary <u>are</u> moving house.

If 'Jack and Mary' were replaced by the pronoun 'they', the plural form of the verb would automatically be used. If you are in doubt, replace the nouns with a pronoun to find the correct form of the verb.

Sometimes a singular noun is followed by a phrase which contains a plural noun. In this case the verb is connected to the singular noun and will therefore be singular.

> The award winning <u>athlete</u>, with all his team mates, <u>was invited</u> to Berlin.

'Athlete' is singular so it is followed by the singular form of the verb, 'was invited'. If both nouns had been incorporated into a noun phrase as the *subject* of the sentence, the plural form of the verb would have been used.

> <u>The award winning athlete and all his team mates were invited</u> to Berlin.

'The award winning athlete and all his team mates' is a noun phrase acting as the subject of the sentence. It is plural so the plural form of the verb follows.

Exceptions
There are some expressions which contain two nouns so closely linked with each other that they are almost inseparable. Because of this, it has become acceptable to use the singular form of the verb. Most of them seem to be involved with food!

> Your <u>fish and chips is</u> on the table.

> <u>Salt and pepper seasons</u> food.

> <u>A roll and butter goes</u> together.

Roast beef and Yorkshire pudding is a traditional Sunday meal.

Bread and butter was handed round.

There is a needle and thread in my workbasket.

If a singular noun is followed by 'of' and a plural noun, the singular verb is used. It is the singular noun that is related to the verb. In the following examples the singular noun and the verb are both underlined.

There is a pile of plates on the table.

That pair of socks belongs to Dan.

The collection of papers has blown out of the window.

His pocketful of coins was jingling.

A pound of pears is very expensive.

PRONOUNS

There is often confusion when two pronouns or a noun and a pronoun are used at the beginning or end of a sentence or clause. When a pronoun is used as an object, its form is different from its use as the subject of the sentence.

Subject	Object
I	me
you	you
he, she, it	him, her, it
we	us
they	them

Peter and <u>I</u> are going shopping.

There are two subjects in this sentence – 'Peter' and 'I'. If you remove 'Peter', you will know that 'I' is the correct pronoun. It would not be:

Peter and <u>me</u> are going shopping.

You would not say, 'Me is going shopping.'

However if the pronoun is used as an object, it is different.

The audience liked my partner and <u>me</u>.

'My partner and me' are the objects of the sentence so in this case the pronoun is 'me'. Remove 'my partner' and you will realise why. You would not say: The audience liked <u>I</u>.

Other examples:

The teacher praised <u>him</u> for his project. (object)

<u>He</u> was praised for his project. (subject)

I gave <u>her</u> some sweets. (object)

She gave <u>me</u> some sweets. (object)

The problem usually arises when there are two subjects or two objects. To check you have the correct word, remove one of them to see if the remaining one sounds right.

TAUTOLOGIES

A **tautology** is when the same thing is said twice in different ways. 'Tauto' is Greek for 'the same'. Tautologies should be avoided as they are unnecessary. Your writing should be clear and you should not need to repeat yourself. If you think carefully about what you wish to say, you will avoid using superfluous words. They will spoil your writing. It is so easy to add an extra adjective for emphasis when all you are doing is repeating yourself.

She picked up the tiny, little baby.

'Tiny' and 'little' mean the same thing. You don't need both.

She cried tears.

Of course she did! We use tautologies often when speaking but the spoken word and the written word are different. When you write, think about your words first and then edit them to get the best sentence. How often have you heard the following expressions?

First and foremost

Each and every one

They are tautologies. *One* of the words is sufficient. Equally absurd are the following:

A round circle	A circle is, of course, round.
An unexpected surprise.	A surprise has to be unexpected.
An old antique picture.	You can hardly have a *new* antique!
A three-cornered triangle.	Of course a triangle is three-cornered.

Looking back in retrospect.	'Looking back' is the same as 'in retrospect'.
Future outlook.	An outlook always looks to the future.
New innovation.	An innovation *is* new.
Final completion.	A completion has to be final.

Look at the following sentences and note the obvious tautologies:

The first chapter started the book.

The students received the prizes one after the other in succession.

The applause was deafening as every member of the audience clapped loudly.

MALAPROPISMS

In Sheridan's play *The Rivals* his character, Mrs Malaprop, loved the sound of long words. Unfortunately she was never sure of their meaning and consequently often used the wrong one. She has given her name to the misuse of words.

A **malapropism** is a word that is used in mistake for one that sounds similar. It usually results in nonsense and Sheridan used it to great effect in his comedy. In the following extract Mrs Malaprop describes the education she would give her daughter if she had one.

She should have a supercilious (superficial) knowledge of accounts. I would have her instructed in geometry (geography) that she might learn something of the contagious (contiguous) countries . . . and that she might reprehend (comprehend) the true meaning of what she is saying. This . . . is what I would have a woman know and I don't think there is a superstitious (superfluous) article in it.

Don't fall into the same trap as Mrs Malaprop!
Check your words in the dictionary.

Confusion of words

The two words 'comprise' and 'compose' are often confused. The verb 'comprise' requires a complement to follow it.

His library <u>comprises</u> a collection of rare books and manuscripts.

The verb 'composed' is usually followed by the preposition 'of'.

His library is <u>composed of</u> rare books and manuscripts.

Following is a list of other words which are often confused.

already (before a time)	all ready (everything prepared)
altogether (on the whole)	all together (everyone together)
always (at all times)	all ways (every way)
amiable (friendly – person)	amicable (pleasant – thing)
anyone (any person)	any one (any particular thing)
complement (thing that completes)	compliment (flattering comment)
council (body of people)	counsel (to advise someone)

disinterested (impartial) uninterested (not interested)
ensure (make sure) assure (give confidence) insure (guarantee)

especially (in particular) specially (for a special purpose)
everyone (all – people) every one (each thing)
fictional (made up story or person) fictitious (untrue)

historic (something of note) historical (relating to history)
practise (verb) practice (noun)
principal (head of college) principle (a moral precept)
prophecy (noun) prophesy (verb)
stationary (not moving) stationery (paper etc.)
wander (to walk around) wonder (to think about)

HOMOPHONES

Homophones are words that sound the same as other words but mean something different and are spelt differently. It is very easy to use the wrong one so do make sure you are correct. Some of the most common are:

there their they're

There (place) is our house.

Their (possessive) luggage is in the coach.

They're (they are) going on a cruise.

here hear

Here (place) is your tea.

I can't hear (verb) you.

allowed aloud

He was allowed (verb) to stay up late.

She spoke <u>aloud</u> (adverb).

   to   two   too

I am going <u>to</u> (preposition) London.

They have <u>two</u> (number) dogs.

It is <u>too</u> (qualifying adverb) hot.

   your   you're

Take <u>your</u> (possessive) lunch with you.

<u>You're</u> (you are) looking very pretty.

Although the pronunciation of *off* and *of* is not identical, the two words are often confused.

He took <u>off</u> (part of the verb: 'to take off') his hat.

This is part <u>of</u> (preposition) the document.

To use *off* and *of* together is incorrect.

She fell <u>off of</u> her horse.

This should be:

She fell <u>off</u> her horse.

HOMONYMS

Homonyms are words that have the same spelling but may be pronounced differently and have different meanings.

bow (noun) a tied ribbon or part of a violin.
bow (verb or noun) To incline the head

calf (noun) fleshy part of the leg below the knee
            a young cow

refuse (noun) rubbish
refuse (verb) to show obstinacy

row (noun) a line or an argument
row (verb) to argue angrily

SPELLING

English spelling is not easy because although there *are* some rules, these are often broken. It is very important therefore to use a dictionary if you are unsure of a word. Check the spelling *and* the meaning.

The Spell Check

The Spell Check on your word processor won't pick up malapropisms or homophones. It will only tell you if words are *spelt* incorrectly. It is a useful tool but it is necessary to read over your work as well and check any words you are not sure about.

SOME COMMON MISTAKES

Following is a list of common mistakes:

◆   It's = it is or it has.

◆ Its possessive does *not* have an apostrophe.

◆ The ending for an adverb of manner is 'ly' *not* 'ley'.

◆ Don't use commas instead of full stops.

◆ 'All right' is the correct spelling. *Not* alright.

◆ 'On to' is two words not one.

◆ Use 'try to' *not* 'try and'.

◆ Use 'while' not 'whilst'.

◆ 'A lot' is two words.

◆ 'In front' is two words.

◆ Do not modify the following words. They stand alone:

excellent   perfect   round   square
triangular   unique

Other common mistakes

'Also', 'then' and 'like' are *not* conjunctions. Put 'and' before 'also' and 'then' in the middle of a sentence.

She went to Paris <u>and also</u> to Bruges.

I did my shopping <u>and then</u> had lunch.

Do not use 'like' as a conjunction. Use 'as if' or 'as though'.

It looks <u>as if</u> it will be sunny.

not

It looks <u>like</u> it will be sunny.

'Like' should be followed by an object (noun or pronoun).

Pat looked <u>like</u> her mother.

Remember to use 'different from' *not* 'different to' or 'different than'.

The job was <u>different from</u> any of my previous posts.

It should be 'bored with' or 'bored by' not 'bored of'.

I am <u>bored with</u> this book.

He was <u>bored by</u> the lecture.

The same applies to the colloquial 'fed up'. It should be 'fed up with' *not* 'fed up of'.

I am fed up <u>with</u> this weather.

not

I am fed up <u>of</u> this weather.

Less and fewer
The word 'less' is often incorrectly used when it should be 'fewer'. 'Less' refers to a measured quantity. 'Fewer' refers to something that is counted.

There should be <u>less</u> sugar in that recipe.

This year there are <u>fewer</u> teachers at the school.

The possessive form
'Theirs' and 'yours' never require an apostrophe. They are possessive pronouns.

> That house is <u>theirs</u>.

> This book is <u>yours</u>.

Giving a reason

A sentence containing the words 'the reason being' is wrong. You do not need to include the word 'being'.

> We are sorry to be late. The reason (being) is that we had an accident.

You could, of course, condense the sentence to:

> We are late because we had an accident.

or

> The reason we are late is that we had an accident.

In some cases 'because' could be replaced by 'that'.

> The reason he was tired was <u>because</u> he had been driving all day.

This could be:

> The reason he was tired was <u>that</u> he had been driving all day.

or

He was tired because he had been driving all day.

Frequently the word 'reason' is superfluous. It is 'understood' through the sense of the sentence.

Double negatives

I have not got no books.

This means you *have* got some books. The 'not' cancels out the 'no'. It should be:

I have <u>not</u> got <u>any</u> books.

or

I <u>have</u> got <u>no</u> books.

The double negative can be used for effect but it should be used sparingly or it will lose its effect.

He was <u>not unkind</u> to her but he showed a lack of care.

This would not have been so effective without the double negative.

It was <u>no little</u> achievement to win the gold medal.

This would have been just as effective as:

It was a great achievement to win the gold medal.

CHECKLIST

◆ Don't use commas instead of full stops.

◆ Make sure your nouns and verbs agree.

◆ Avoid tautologies and malapropisms.

◆ Avoid double negatives.

◆ Check your work carefully.

EXERCISE

Correct and punctuate the following passage:

The government are planning a referendum about a common currency neither the labour nor the conservative party have spoken a great deal about it as their have been alot of other events to occupy there time recently they have been to busy too talk to their constituents about it many MPs have been abroad and each and everyone have been on holiday from westminster when they return it is hoped they will here what the people are saying parliament is very different to the parliament of too hundred years ago today it comprises of both men and women peers and they will attend the opening of parliament in november they have to be present they cannot give no reasons for not attending.

See page 168 for suggested answers.

Style

You have now been shown how to vary your sentence construction. Your sentences should be organised into paragraphs and you must plan your work before you start writing. Decide what is to go into each paragraph.

PARAGRAPHING

A **paragraph** consists of several sentences dealing with one topic. Your work should always be broken up into paragraphs. If it is one long piece with no paragraphs, it will be very difficult to read. Each paragraph should be indented so that the reader is aware you are starting afresh. (For typed letters and single spaced typing a space can be left between the paragraphs instead of indenting. However, this should *not* be done in hand-written work.)

Each paragraph should be related in some way to the one before it and the one after it.

The topic sentence

The **topic sentence** is the main sentence in the paragraph. The other sentences expand on it. Its positioning in the sentence can vary. In the following example it comes at the beginning and the rest of the sentences tell you more about it.

Kate sat dejectedly in the airport lounge and stared around her. Two teenagers were chattering excitedly about their proposed holiday. A mother was tearfully bidding good-bye to her daughter while her husband stood beside her. A small boy was zooming around making loud aeroplane noises. All of them seemed to have purpose in their lives except her.

The topic sentence which starts the paragraph sets the scene and we are then told more detail in the following sentences. The last one leads naturally on to the following paragraph which will explain why Kate is depressed.

She should have been so happy. A man walked by and she looked up, startled. For a moment she had thought it was Mark. She wondered what he was doing now. Was he thinking of her? Tears flooded her eyes. Tomorrow should have been her wedding day.

In this paragraph the sentence leads up to the topic sentence at the end. It sums up the previous sentences and suggests that the following paragraph will give reasons for the cancelled wedding. Sometimes the topic sentence will be in the middle with the opening sentences preparing the ground-work and the following ones continuing to expand it.

She should have known something was wrong when he so often worked late. He had frequently made excuses for not meeting her. However, she was unprepared for the stark message left on her answer phone. He had told her bluntly that he was going to marry her best friend. He hoped she would understand and they could remain friends. She could still hear every word. It was burnt into her memory for ever.

The first two sentences build up to the answer phone message and the ones after the topic sentence expand it.

The single sentence paragraph

It is important to vary the length of your paragraphs. Occasionally you can use a single sentence paragraph but don't use it too often. It is sometimes used for dramatic effect.

Kate was relaxing in the drawing room with a book when she heard the front door bell. Idly she speculated about the visitor. It was no doubt someone for her aunt. After all no one knew where she was. She heard the door behind her open and her aunt's voice informing her she had a visitor. Turning quickly, she gasped.

Mark stood in the doorway, looking sheepish.

In the previous example the single sentence paragraph stands out starkly after the build up to it in the previous paragraph.

Your opening paragraph should provide an introduction to your work and the last one a conclusion. Make sure the opening sentences are interesting so the reader will want to read on. Your paragraphs should work for you. Vary the length and change the position of the topic sentence. Make sure that one paragraph leads naturally on to the next. Use the single sentence paragraph sparingly. Remember that dialogue has specific rules for paragraphing. Each speaker starts the speech at the beginning of a new paragraph.

JARGON

'**Jargon**' derives from a Middle English word meaning 'meaningless chatter'. It is described in the Oxford dictionary as 'unintelligible words, gibberish'. It has come to mean language used by a particular group of people – lawyers, teachers, politicians and others. Some 'jargon' words have become common usage. Words ending in '-ise' have become embedded in our language:

finalise   prioritise   privatise   normalise

If you are a member of a particular group, you may be tempted to use your 'in' jargon at other times. Guard against this. Remember that the words and expressions will probably only be intelligible to other members of your group.

> **Avoid using jargon**.

CLICHÉS

You should also avoid **clichés** in your writing. These are expressions that have been used over and over again. They were original when used for the first time – probably by Shakespeare or in the Bible.

He stopped dead in his tracks.

She went as white as a sheet.

I can see it in my mind's eye. (Shakespeare)

All that glitters (glisters) is not gold. (Shakespeare)

There's nothing new under the sun. (The Bible)

Don't hide your light under a bushel. (The Bible)

It is very easy to use clichés because they are so well known and often seem exactly right. But it is better to create your own original expression.

> **Avoid clichés. Create your own expressions.**

COLLOQUIAL LANGUAGE

Colloquial language is language that is used in speech or when writing informally. It should be avoided in formal writing. It is not always easy to distinguish between colloquialisms and slang. One dictionary may classify a word as colloquial while another may regard it as slang. Slang is the most extreme type of informal language.

When writing formally, avoid colloquialisms and slang although they are permissible in your dialogue. Occasionally you may wish to use a colloquial word in your formal work to create a particular effect. In this case enclose it in inverted commas.

CHOICE OF WORDS

As well as making sure your grammar and punctuation are accurate, you should think carefully about your choice of words before you write. This is why planning any piece of work you do is essential.

Make your writing 'tight' by avoiding repetition and making sure you don't use several words if one will do. Delete unnecessary adverbs of manner. Your verb should frequently be sufficient to indicate *how* something is done.

She <u>ran quickly</u> out of the room.

This would be more effective if you used the verb 'rushed'.

She <u>rushed</u> out of the room.

Don't use tautologies which are simply repetition or malapropisms (words that sound similar to other words but are used incorrectly)!

VARYING YOUR STYLE

You will have to adapt your style of writing to the particular work you are doing. A newspaper report will not be the same as a short story. The report of a football match will differ from a true account of an exciting incident. Read widely to enlarge your vocabulary and notice how other writers use language. Don't copy them. Learn from them but develop your own style. Write frequently and your style will improve.

CHECKLIST

◆ A paragraph deals with one topic.

◆ Use the single sentence paragraph sparingly.

◆ Avoid jargon, clichés and colloquialisms in formal writing.

EXERCISES

Write a short story or an article using one of the following titles:

- ◆ Lost!

- ◆ Remembering Yesterday

- ◆ A Childhood Memory

- ◆ The Journey

- ◆ The Visit

- ◆ Escape!

- ◆ The Hostage

Revision

This chapter is a revision one to reinforce what you have learnt.

PARTS OF SPEECH
Each word is a part of speech which has a role to play in your sentence.

Nouns
Concrete or **common nouns** are the names of things:

book   table

Proper nouns are the names of people or places and always start with a capital letter:

Alison   England

Abstract nouns are states or feelings: beauty   happiness

Collective nouns are singular words which refer to a group of objects or people:

team   crowd   audience

Gerunds are verb-nouns formed from the present participle of the verb:

crying   shopping

Articles

The articles are the words: the   a   an

'The' is the **definite article** used for specific items.

'A' and 'an' are more general. 'An' is used before a vowel. These are the **indefinite articles**.

Pronouns

Pronouns take the place of nouns:

the boy	he
my brother and I	we

Relative pronouns link clauses:

This is the girl who stole the book.

Verbs

Verbs are 'doing' or 'being' words. **Finite verbs** are 'completed' verbs which show person, number and tense.

She threw the ball.

'Threw' is the finite verb; 'she' is the third person singular (number) and the tense is the past.

The **non-finite verbs** are:

the infinitive	to do	to jump
present participle (always ends in '-ing')	doing	jumping
past participle (used with verb to have)	He had <u>done</u>.	
	She has <u>jumped</u>.	

Adjectives

Adjectives qualify nouns. They either precede the noun or follow the verb 'to be'.

I will use the <u>blue</u> counter.

My counter is <u>blue</u>.

Adverbs

Adverbs qualify verbs, adjectives and other adverbs.

She laughed <u>happily</u>. (Adverb of manner qualifying verb 'laughed'.)

He was <u>very</u> handsome. (Adverb qualifying adjective 'handsome'.)

They ran <u>very</u> quickly to the scene. (Adverb qualifying adverb 'quickly'.)

Conjunctions

Conjunctions link clauses: because   while   when   if

You can go out <u>when</u> it stops raining.

Prepositions

Prepositions show the relationship between one word and another:

The bird flew <u>into</u> the room.

Interjections

Interjections are expressions showing an emotion. They are not necessary to the sentence.

Oh!   Goodness me!

SENTENCE CONSTRUCTION

A sentence *must* contain at least one noun or pronoun, which is the subject of the sentence, and a finite verb.

Clauses

There are two types of clause – main and subordinate. Each sentence must contain at least one main clause. A clause contains *one* finite verb. Subordinate clauses can be linked to main clauses by the use of conjunctions. If you have more than one finite verb in a sentence, you have more than one clause. Check that you have linked the clauses with conjunctions.

She was crying because her mother had punished her.

She was crying	(main clause)
her mother had punished her	(subordinate clause)
because	(conjunction)

Do not put a comma between two main clauses unless you are writing a *list* of main clauses. Remember that the last one *must* be preceded by 'and'.

Jack switched on the computer, picked up his notes, keyed in his password and started typing.

Phrases

Phrases are groups of words that do not contain a finite verb and can be used to add detail to a sentence.

Running across the road, she embraced her sister.

Running across the road (participial phrase)

He carefully placed the evidence on the table.

on the table   (prepositional phrase)

PUNCTUATION MARKS

The full stop

Never use a comma instead of a full stop. Put the latter when your sentence is completed, checking that you have linked your clauses appropriately. A full stop can also be used after abbreviations but *not* contractions.

The comma

Use a comma for the following purposes:

◆ To separate items or clauses in a list remembering the last one must be preceded by 'and'.

◆ To separate the subordinate clause from the main clause when you start your sentence with a conjunction.

◆ To separate dialogue from the person who is speaking.

◆ To separate adjectival clauses in the middle of a main clause.

◆ To separate phrases from the rest of the clause.

◆ Before or after a name when the person concerned is being addressed.

◆ Before expressions like 'will you?' 'haven't you?'

The semicolon
A semicolon is not as strong as a full stop and can be used to separate main clauses if one follows closely on to the first. You can also use it if a list of things or people follow it.

The colon
A colon can also be used to introduce a list and to expand the previous sentence. It is sometimes used to reinforce the previous sentence. A colon is also used after the character's name when writing a play.

The exclamation mark
Use the exclamation mark if you have written the word 'exclaimed' but be wary of its use at other times. Don't use it too much or its effect will be lost.

The question mark
Do remember to put a question mark at the end of a question even if it is a rhetorical one (one that does not require an answer).

APOSTROPHES

The apostrophe has two uses.

Possession

The apostrophe is used to show that a noun has something belonging to it. Usually if the noun is singular, the apostrophe goes *before* the 's' and if it is plural, it goes *after* the 's'.

The boy's coat.

The boys' playground.

The exception is when the noun does not need an 's' to make it plural. In this case the apostrophe goes *before* the 's' which is added.

The children's clothes.

The mice's tails.

Abbreviations

The apostrophe is also used when a letter is omitted. The apostrophe is placed instead of the missing letter or letters.

could not	couldn't
have not	haven't
might have	might've

PARAGRAPHS

Remember to arrange your sentences in paragraphs. Each one should deal with one topic and there should be a topic sentence to introduce it or sum it up. Use single sentence paragraphs occasionally for effect.

DIALOGUE

Direct speech

Direct speech should be enclosed in inverted commas. A new paragraph is started for each speaker. Use a comma to separate the speech from the speaker. If a speaker speaks for several paragraphs, open the inverted commas at the beginning of each paragraph but do not close them until the speech is completed.

Indirect speech

Indirect speech is reporting what someone has said and therefore inverted commas are not required. The first person is usually changed to the third and the present tense to the past.

Writing a play

Inverted commas are not needed when writing a play. Put a colon after the character's name. Put stage directions in brackets (or in italics if typing).

CHECKLIST

◆ Each part of speech has a role to play in the sentence.

◆ Each sentence must contain at least one main clause.

◆ Make sure clauses are linked correctly.

◆ Do not use a comma instead of a full stop.

◆ Write in paragraphs.

EXERCISE

Correct and punctuate the following passage:

I don't want to be married in church exclaimed sarah nonsense dear of course you do everyone wants a white wedding in church her mother replied st pauls church will be perfect with its beautiful porch its setting is ideal it would of been alright if i was ten years younger but im thirty and i dont want to go to church it would be hypocritical well have to make a guest list her mother ignored her when are we going to meet james parents i shall need a list of guests from them to sarah clenched her fists mother i dont want a big church wedding james and i want a quiet wedding with no fuss her mother wasnt listening she was already making plans sarah flounced out of the room slamming the door what are we going to do she said to james that evening my parents want a big white wedding all i want is to slip away quietly with you and get married i thought youd like to choose the childrens dresses teased james to match your beautiful white gown what children my nieces of course there longing to be bridesmaids oh dear sighed sarah id forgotten about them and my parents want to meet yours do you think thats a good idea theyll have to meet sometime replied james are you serious about wanting a quiet wedding of course i am then lets run away to gretna green.

See page 168–9 for suggested answers.

The Dictionary and Thesaurus

If you are serious about improving your standard of writing, a dictionary and a thesaurus are useful books to have beside you.

THE DICTIONARY

The dictionary contains a vast amount of information and it can be a fascinating experience to browse through it if you have time.

The first dictionaries

The first major dictionary was produced by Dr Samuel Johnson in 1755. There had been earlier ones but they were very rudimentary. The first ones were produced by monks in the fifteenth century. Latin was the traditional language of the mediaeval church and the monks tried to find English equivalents for Latin words. Dr Johnson had a reputation as a man of learning and, unlike some of his contemporaries in the eighteenth century, he recognised that language is constantly changing. Today, with the advent of new technology and the consequent increase of new words, dictionaries have to be constantly updated.

Derivations of words

English is a difficult language to learn because it derives from so many different languages. Latin has already been mentioned and many Latin words and phrases are still in use today.

curriculum vitae	– an account of one's career
et cetera	– and so on
in camera	– not in open court
infra dig	– beneath one's dignity
in memoriam	– in memory
nota bene	– note well
rigor mortis	– the stiffening of a corpse

William the Conqueror brought the French language to these shores in 1066. In spite of reaction by the Anglo-Saxon natives, French words and phrases crept into the English language. Some are still in use today.

à la carte	– separate items on a menu
au gratin	– cooked in breadcrumbs and grated cheese
avant-garde	– new progressive ideas
corps diplomatique	– diplomatic corps
deja vu	– a sense of having experienced something before
en masse	– all together
fait accompli	– something done that cannot be changed

mot juste	– the right word
table d'hôte	– fixed price menu
petit mal	– mild form of epilepsy
pot-pourri	– a mixture
rendezvous	– a meeting

Because the English travelled the world, words from many other languages have been incorporated into the English language. Words that derive from other languages are identified in the dictionary. You will find a list of abbreviations in the front of your dictionary. Among them will be foreign languages. Here are four words that derive from other languages.

Hottentot	Afrikaans (Afrik.)
hour	Greek (Gk)
sabre	Polish (Pol.)
shawl	Persian (Pers.)

Parts of speech

Your dictionary will classify each word as a particular part of speech. Remember that some words can be more than one part of speech depending on the way they are used in the sentence. Some dictionaries will give examples. Below is a list of the usual abbreviations used for parts of speech with definitions given also for revision purposes.

Noun (n.)	– a person, place, thing, state or idea
Pronoun (pron.)	– a word that replaces a noun

Verb (v.t.)	– a transitive verb that takes an object
Verb (v.i.)	– an intransitive verb that doesn't take an object
Adjective (a.)	– a word that describes a noun
Adverb (adv.)	– a word that qualifies a verb, an adjective or another adverb
Conjunction (conj.)	– a word that joins two clauses in a sentence
Preposition (prep.)	– a word that shows the relationship between one word and another
Interjection (int.)	– an exclamation

Pronunciation

The dictionary will also indicate on which syllable the stress is placed and this will help you with pronunciation. Most dictionaries use 'received pronunciation', the standard English with no accent associated with speakers from the South of England. Regional dialects are ignored although sometimes American pronunciation is mentioned.

Definitions

On most occasions you will use your dictionary to check the spelling or the meaning of a word. Many words have more than one meaning and the dictionary separates them clearly. Most dictionaries will also have an appendix at the back containing new words or words that have been omitted from the main part of the dictionary.

Prefixes and Suffixes

A **prefix** is a group of letters placed in front of a root word to change the meaning.

appear	disappear	dependent	independent
happy	unhappy	script	postscript

A **suffix** is a group of letters placed *after* the root word. This also changes the meaning.

beauty	beautiful	bright	brightness	
dark	darkness	hope	hopeless	hopeful

Both prefixes and suffixes will be found in most dictionaries and they are usually followed by a list of words in which they are used.

Hyphens

The dictionary will also indicate where hyphens are necessary but not all sources agree on their inclusion in particular words.

Portmanteau words

Portmanteau words are words formed by the combination of two other words. Lewis Carroll is credited with creating this one in his book *Alice Through the Looking Glass*.

chortle — from chuckle and snort

Portmanteau words are very popular today.

brunch — from breakfast and lunch

motel — from motor and hotel

Oxbridge — from Oxford and Cambridge

THE THESAURUS

A **thesaurus** is a very useful book. It contains a number of **synonyms** (words which have a similar meaning to another word). If you can't find the right word or you have repeated a word too many times, a thesaurus will help you find an alternative.

It was Peter Mark Roget who produced the first thesaurus. He was a professor of physiology who helped to found the University of London. He completed the first draft of a thesaurus for his own use in 1806 and added to it over the next forty years. When he retired in 1840, he continued to work on it and his final work was published by Longmans in 1852. The book was very popular and during his lifetime twenty-eight editions were published. After his death, his son and then his grandson continued his work.

Roget's Thesaurus, as it has become known, is still in use and is frequently updated. Today there are many other thesauri on the market including small pocket editions. It is certainly worthwhile to invest in one. You will find it an invaluable aid.

CHECKLIST

◆ A dictionary gives parts of speech, pronunciation, definitions and derivations.

◆ A thesaurus consists of a collection of synonyms.

◆ Use a dictionary and a thesaurus to help you widen your vocabulary.

Answers to Exercises

CHAPTER 1

1. Plurals:

cats	crutches	children	deer
duchesses	dwarfs–dwarves	halves	ladies
men	marriages	metaphors	similes

2. Concrete or common nouns:

town	theatre	actors	
café	coffee	umbrella	stand

Proper noun: Jenny

Abstract nouns: depression   therapy   past

Collective noun: audience

Gerund: shopping

Finite verbs:

decided	had suffered	had been
had collapsed	would be	had helped

started	went	left	
were	could (not)	remember	was

Personal pronouns: she   it

Demonstrative pronoun: that

Possessive pronoun: hers

Interrogative pronoun: which

3. Finite verbs:

was   wanted   was raining   looked   picked up could do

Non-finite verbs:

Infinitive:	to play	to see
Present participle:		staring
Past participle:	bored	annoyed

4. Complements: (e) inspector   (f) a good swimmer

Direct objects: (a) a library book   (b) several letters (c) an ice cream   (d) an apple

Indirect objects: (a) Jack   (d) him

5. Transitive verbs: (b) gave   (c) threw

Intransitive verbs: (a) cried   (d) is . . . talking

6. Passive voice:

(a) The guest of honour was served first by the hostess.

(b) Night storage heaters were installed by the landlord for his tenants.

CHAPTER 2

1. Linking sentences

(a) Elaine, who taught English, was a popular teacher and had worked at the same school for many years.

(b) Clive was in a furious temper because his computer had crashed and he had to complete some work in a hurry.

(c) It was a beautiful day, the sun was shining, the birds were singing, the flowers were smiling and Helen felt glad to be alive.

(d) The old lady put her hand on the shelf but it collapsed and she fell heavily, bruising her face.

(e) The book launch was scheduled for October but it was postponed until November because the printer had not finished printing the books.

2. Identifying phrases and clauses

(a) . . . she flung the book . . .   main clause
. . . on the table . . .   prepositional phrase/ adverbial phrase

(b) The student wriggled his way . . .   main clause
. . . into the pothole.   prepositional phrase/ adverbial phrase

(c) He yearned to fly on Concorde.   main clause
. . . to fly on Concorde   infinitive phrase

(d) Dreaming of her holiday . . .   noun phrase using a
                                           gerund (subject of
                                           sentence)
    (it) made her forget . . .   main clause

(e) Furiously angry . . .   adjectival phrase
    . . . she shouted at her   main clause
    daughter . . .

(f) They have gone on holiday.   main clause
    . . . on holiday   prepositional phrase/
                                           adverbial phrase

(g) To visit Australia was his   main clause
    ambition.
    . . . to visit Australia . . .   infinitive phrase

(h) The postponed match . . .   noun phrase
                                           (subject of sentence)
    (it) was to take place   main clause
    . . . the following day   adverbial phrase

(i) Gazing out of the window . . .   participial phrase
    . . . he wondered . . .   main clause
    . . . he should do next . . .   noun clause
                                           (object of wondered)

(j) Hurrying to catch her train . . .   participial phrase
    . . . Denise tripped and fell heavily. main clause

3. Identifying the subordinate clauses

. . . had been badly beaten . . .   – adjectival clause
                                           modifying 'prisoner'.

. . . he was climbing out of the   – adverbial clause of
window . . .   time

. . . the terrorists had been   – adverbial clause of
hiding . . .   place

. . . a meeting had been arranged . . .	– adverbial clause of reason
. . . he had stayed in his hotel . . .	– adverbial clause of condition
. . . as hard as he could . . .	– adverbial clause of degree
. . . something was done . . .	– adverbial clause of condition

4. Subjunctive:

(a) If I <u>were</u> a giant, I could reach that shelf.

(b) If she <u>were</u> to ask me, I would go.

CHAPTER 3

1. Phrases and clauses

(a) The match was cancelled . . .	main clause
. . . of the weather . . .	prepositional phrase
(b) We can go . . .	main clause
. . . you are ready.	adverbial clause of time
(c) The policeman chased the thief . . .	main clause
. . . caught him . . .	main clause
. . . handcuffed him . . .	main clause
. . . took him to the police station . . .	main clause
. . . to charge him . . .	infinitive phrase
(d) Leaping out of the car . . .	participial phrase
. . . she dashed into the shop . . .	main clause

(e) Julie was doing her homework . . .   main clause
    . . . Dan was laying the table . . .   main clause
    . . . their father was reading the paper . . .   main clause
    . . . their mother was preparing diner . . .   main clause

2. Punctuation

George leapt out of bed, stubbing his toe on the chair which was beside him. Hobbling to the window, he stared gloomily out. It was raining. Perhaps it would brighten up later. He watched the milkman drive down the road. He was late. Sleepily he drifted into the bathroom to wash and shave. He cursed as he cut himself. Dabbing the blood with a piece of cotton wool, he wondered how he would perform at his interview. He must not be late.

CHAPTER 4

1. Adjectives:

beautiful	no	long	cliff	two
picturesque	welcome	some	sore	glad
attractive	wooden	small	only	distant
peaceful				

2. Adverbs:

dreamily (manner)   lazily (manner)   carefully (manner)
happily (manner)   too (qualifying adjective 'late')
soon (time)   so (degree)   around (place)
abroad (place)   very (qualifying adjective 'country')
so (qualifying adverb 'much')   much (degree)

CHAPTER 5

Punctuation

David flung open the office door and sat down at his desk; he had a great deal to do. Would he complete the report in time? He knew he should not have left it till the last moment. Switching on the computer, he keyed in the password and started to list the items to be included: the statement from the assessors, the secretary's report, the year's accounts and the government's recommendations. Crash! He started. What was that? Rushing to the window, he looked out. Two men – or was it more – were running across the road.

CHAPTER 6

Apostrophes

John's parents were going on a week's holiday. While they were away, he would stay at his grandparents' house. He hoped they'd take him to the children's adventure playground. He would go on lots of rides. His mother's dog would be put in the kennels while they were away. His friend's family was going on a month's holiday to America. John had been very envious of Ben's new suitcase.

His parents and Ben's parents took the two boys out for a meal before they left. John noticed that the waitress's stockings were laddered. He didn't like some of the food on the menu but eventually decided on the 'chef's special'. He would've liked a hamburger but it was not available.

CHAPTER 7

1. Dialogue

Alan stared at his wife in dismay.

'Are you sure you're pregnant?' he asked.

'Of course I'm sure,' she replied crossly.

'But we agreed we couldn't afford a baby yet. Did you forget to take the pill?'

'I suppose I must have done.'

'What are we going to do about it?' he queried.

'There's nothing we can do.'

'Of course there is.'

'I won't have an abortion if that's what you mean. I might've agreed once but not now.'

'But how can we afford to keep a child?' he said in exasperation. 'We can hardly afford to keep ourselves.'

'Don't be so ridiculous,' Kate scoffed. 'I'm going to read the pamphlet the doctor gave me. It's called "Baby Care".'

She left the room before he could reply.

2. Play form:

(Enter Alan and his wife, Kate)

Alan: Are you sure you're pregnant?

Kate: Of course I'm sure.

Alan: But we agreed we couldn't afford a baby yet. Did you forget to take the pill?

Kate: I suppose I must have done.

Alan: What are we going to do about it?

Kate: There's nothing we can do.

Alan: Of course there is.

Kate: I won't have an abortion if that's what you mean. I might've agreed once but not now.

Alan: But how can we afford to keep a child? We can hardly afford to keep ourselves.

Kate: Don't be so ridiculous. I'm going to read the pamphlet the doctor gave me. It's called *Baby Care*. (Exit)

CHAPTER 8

Correction:

The government is planning a referendum about a common currency. Neither the Labour nor the Conservative party has spoken a great deal about it as there have been a lot of other events to occupy their time. Recently they have been too busy to talk to their constituents about it. Many MPs have been abroad and each one has been on holiday from Westminster. When they return, it is hoped they will hear what the people are saying. Parliament is very different from the parliament of two hundred years ago. Today it comprises both men and women peers and they will attend the opening of Parliament in November. They have to be present. They cannot give reasons for not attending.

CHAPTER 10

Punctuation

'I don't want to be married in church!' exclaimed Sarah.

'Nonsense, dear. Of course you do; everyone wants a white wedding in church,' her mother replied. 'St Paul's Church will be perfect with its beautiful porch. Its setting is ideal.'

'It would've been all right if I was ten years younger. But I'm thirty and I don't want to go to church. It would be hypocritical.'

'We'll have to make a guest list.' Her mother ignored her. 'When are we going to meet James' parents? I shall need a list of guests from them too.'

Sarah clenched her fists. 'Mother, I don't want a big church wedding. James and I want a quiet wedding with no fuss.'

Her mother wasn't listening. She was already making plans. Sarah flounced out of the room slamming the door.

'What are we going to do?' she said to James that evening. 'My parents want a big white wedding. All I want is to slip away quietly with you and get married.'

'I thought you'd like to choose the children's dresses,' teased James, 'to match your beautiful white gown.'

'What children?'

'My nieces, of course. They're longing to be bridesmaids.'

'Oh dear,' sighed Sarah. 'I'd forgotten about them. And my parents want to meet yours. Do you think that's a good idea?'

'They'll have to meet some time,' replied James. 'Are you serious about wanting a quiet wedding?'

'Of course I am.'

'Then let's run away to Gretna Green.'

Glossary

Acronym. A word formed from the initial letters of other words.

Active voice. The subject *does* the action.

Adjective. A word that describes a noun.

Adverb. A word that qualifies a verb, an adjective or another adverb.

Clause. main: A group of words that contain both a subject and a verb and make sense by themselves.

   subordinate: A group of words containing a verb that depends on the main clause. They cannot stand alone.

Cliché. A well worn saying.

Conjunction. A word that links two clauses together.

Gerund. A present participle used as a noun.

Homophone. A word that is pronounced the same as another but spelt differently.

Interjection. An exclamation.

Inverted commas. Speech marks: These are marks put around speech and quotations.

Jargon. Words or expressions used by a particular group of people.

Malapropism. A word used incorrectly instead of a similar sounding one.

Noun. abstract: A word that denotes a quality or state.

collective. A singular word which refers to a group of people or things.

concrete: The name of a thing.

proper: The name of a person or place.

Object. A noun or pronoun that follows the verb and is related to the subject.

Paragraph. A group of sentences dealing with the same topic.

Passive voice. Something is *done to* the subject.

Phrase. A group of words not necessarily containing a verb or making sense on its own.

Prefix. Letters placed *before* the root word to change the meaning.

Preposition. A word that governs a noun or pronoun.

Pronoun. demonstrative: It takes the place of a noun but is general not personal.

This, these, that, those

interrogative: A pronoun that is used at the start of a question.

personal: A *personal* word that takes the place of a noun.

I, you, he, she, it, we, they

possessive: Used when something belongs.

relative: This has a similar role to a conjunction. It joins clauses together but is closely linked to a noun.

Subject. The noun or pronoun on which the rest of the clause depends.

Suffix. Letters placed *after* the root word to change the meaning.

Summary. A shortened version of a longer piece of writing.

Synonym. A word that can be used to replace another.

Syntax. The way words are combined to form sentences.

Tautology. A statement that is repeated in a different way in the same sentence.

Thesaurus. A book which will give a selection of synonyms.

Topic sentence. The main sentence in a paragraph. This is elaborated in the rest of the paragraph.

Verb. intransitive: A verb that *is not* followed by an object.

  transitive: A verb that *is* followed by an object.

Further Reading

Write Right, Jan Venolia (David St John Publisher)
The King's English, Fowler (Oxford)
Roget's Thesaurus (Longman)
Write On, Richard Bell and Pauline Bentley (Writers News)
English Grammar, B. A. Phythian A. A., M. Litt. (Hodder & Stoughton)
Correct English, B. A. Phythian M. A., M. Litt. (Hodder & Stoughton)
Improve Your Written English, Marion Field (How To Books)

For more advanced students
Mastering Advanced English Language, Sara Thorne (Macmillan)

For light reading
The King's English, Kingsley Amis (Harper Collins)

Index